**Future
Architecture
Platform**

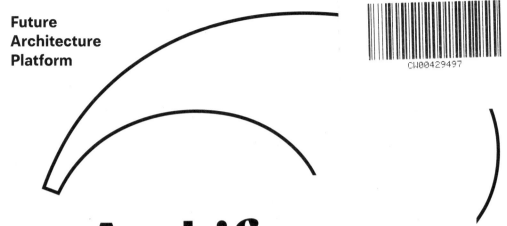

Archifutures

The Site

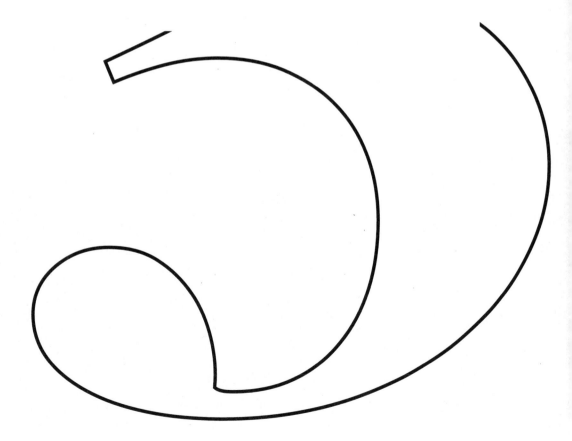

Archifutures

Volume 3: The Site

Future Architecture platform

Archifutures

Volume 3: The Site

A field guide to the future
of architecture

dpr-barcelona   edited by &beyond

Preface

Welcome to *Archifutures Volume 3: The Site,* the third part in a new series of field guides to the future of architecture.

Archifutures maps new developments in the fields of contemporary architecture and urban planning with contributions from institutions, activists, thinkers, curators, architects, urban bloggers, polemicists, critics and editors involved with the Future Architecture platform. Through conversations and essays, interviews and images, across three volumes – *The Museum, The Studio, The Site* – the series lays out an inspiring range of active strategies for the future of the built environment. Both real and imaginary, these are the projects and people shaping tomorrow's architecture and cities.

The *Archifutures* publication series accompanies the Future Architecture platform, a European-wide network and EU-funded initiative set up by the Museum of Architecture and Design in Ljubljana, Slovenia in 2015.

The focus of each of the first three volumes of *Archifutures* is as follows:

Vol. 1: The Museum – a field guide to communicating the future of architecture

Change comes through communicating great ideas. This first volume in the *Archifutures* series looks at communication strategies and education programmes developed by the collaborating institutions and organisations of the Future Architecture platform.

Vol. 2: The Studio – a field guide to speculating upon the future of architecture

If you want to change the world, you need to start with great ideas. This second volume lays out key theories, concepts and manifestos currently forming the architectural horizon.

Vol. 3: The Site – a field guide to making the future of architecture

Why aim to change the world, if you can't translate great ideas into reality? This third volume in the Archifutures series looks at the practical projects, strategies and tools for the future that will transform the landscape of architecture.

Welcome to the future of architecture.
&beyond
October 2016

Contents

Introduction

This, the third volume in the *Archifutures* series of field guides mapping the future of architecture, is focused on *The Site*, and it is a call to action. Containing sixteen of the most inspirational proposals, strategies and projects sent in to and selected by the members of the Future Architecture platform in response to their call for ideas at the end of 2015 – and coming from practitioners, architects and designers from around Europe and beyond – these are practical solutions that could be shaping and making that future on a site near you soon.

In *Volume 1: The Museum*, the spotlight was firmly on the Future Architecture platform members themselves, mapping their strategies as institutions and organisations involved in the communication and support of the latest thought, theory and practice of those leading architecture today.

Volume 2 The Studio then presented a first tranche of essays and interviews from these innovators and others, focusing in particular on the cutting-edge thinking and theory that's framing and scoping out (possible) architecture futures today.

Now this third volume, *The Site*, presents a further selection from the call for ideas with the focus this time firmly on the nitty-gritty of practice: projects and strategies that are on-site or site-ready to shake up that future.

Together the contributions presented here can be seen to represent a collective rolling up of architectural sleeves: projects that are about getting on with the task in hand, getting hands dirty to make a better world. They act as a signal call of a new generation of architects not content to accept the status-quo as it is – the poverty and inequity which seems to have become hardwired into how so many of our cities and societies have developed today, questioning what it is means to be an architect and reasserting the agency of what architecture in its widest sense can contribute, not just to the debate but to helping change things for the better.

In the context of the call to arms, however woolly, of *Reporting from the Front*, the 2016 Venice Architecture Biennale curated by Alejandro Aravena – that demanded a return to an architecture focused on the human condition "as a way to improve people's quality of life" and for architects to be "scrutinising the horizon looking for new fields of action" – much of the work presented here can be seen to reflect this new engagement. Practitioners reporting from the many fronts where architecture in its widest sense can make a difference, whilst also remaking what it means to practice architecture today.

And given the buffeting winds of uncertainty, and the present breakdown of past sureties – driven by technology, economics, politics and toxic cocktails of all three – in a time not of things given but of things not, post-truth, post-digital, post any consensus on what can be done – it is the anger, yet ultimately positivity, of the projects presented here that is heartening: the hapticity of creating a better place in the world, a dwelling, that "room of one's own" which architecture can make.

One of the key points coming out from many of the contributions is that what we do right now matters – so what are contained here are action points for now. For the seeds to making the future better through architecture, start here.

In no work is this clearer than that of the experimental research collective, URBZ (p. 24), whose experience on projects improving conditions in informal settlements around the world, including their work in the slums of Mumbai, informs the piece written by its two founders Matias Echanove and Rahul Srivastava. They passionately argue that the most radical and optimistic act an architect can do is not to plan a perfect utopian solution, but to work out a real problem on the ground, to

improve conditions in neighbourhoods and for communities as they are
developing now.

Filipe Estrela and Sara Neves (p. 66) similarly outline their hands-on
projects in rural Bihar in India, where they've been working with local
villagers to develop a flexible housing model that radically improves living
conditions, while still drawing on local materials and skills – making
architecture which is about the whole life-cycle of a building and not just
static form-making.

This emphasis on utilising resources that already exist – in other words:
not reinventing the wheel but adapting and updating it – infuses several
other of the contributions too. This can include the reutilisation of the
key resource of existing buildings themselves: abandoned or derelict
structures, which unlock strands of local culture and meaning that
are already embedded in the built landscape, something seen clearly
in the work of Ignacio Gias from Spain. His project (p. 170) proposes
imaginatively to renovate the *hórreos* of Northern Spain – old, out-dated
and disused farm storage buildings – for use as the basis of a new network
of cultural tourism and economic revival in the region.

Similarly, Slovenian architect Andrej Strehovec (p. 126), shows how more
temporary, ephemeral inflatable living spaces – or "capsules" as he calls
them – inserted into the carcasses of disused buildings, could quickly
and cheaply repurpose them where previously they would have been too
expensive to restore, giving sustainability to rural and other communities.

Utopian tabula rasa projects are noticeable by their absence here, with
urban proposals looking not at instant transformation but at supporting
a socially informed evolution of cities, improving quality of life through
sustainable urban revival or thoughtful new architecture. For instance
Natasha Reid's creative solution (p. 114) to London's housing crisis is to
recast the traditional townhouse typology into a mixed-use, communal
set of facilities better suited to that city's increasingly diverse needs and

population – flexibly underpinning and maintaining a healthy social mix. Aleksandra Zarek (p. 178) meanwhile outlines her integrated approach to the rejuvenation of whole city districts rather than just through the isolated renovations of individual buildings, making for a much more holistic, sustainable urban evolution in cities, both physically and socially.

Reigniting the ambition and the passion seen in the past in the development of our cities and their improvement for the mutual good – not just in their visible superstructures but in their invisible and often overlooked infrastructures – is what informs Manon Mollard's contribution (p. 92). She speculates on how a city like London could re-harness the flows and structures of the water systems that keep it serviced and dry – echoing how they were once such a powerful a force for good and a symbol of modernity and pride when laid out in the nineteenth century.

Meanwhile it's the other, often faceless, sometimes even pernicious, veiled or hidden systems which underpin the development and look of our cities and spaces – the structures of state-power, of politics and finance – that are the driver behind several other contributions. These uncover how architecture is itself both an expression and tool of these systems, but also how it can also be used to subvert, critique and reveal them, not just as a passive product but an active condition of resistance.

Thus in his contribution, Léopold Lambert (p. 102) exposes and analyses the inherent violence that forms and informs our built environment – the spatial consequence of the politics of the state – from border posts and walls to the police stations of Northern France.

And it is in the context of the stranglehold of extreme land-values in the property market that the neoliberal financial system has created, where Jack Self (p. 48) proposes a provocative project, showing how architects, rather than being sidelined, could become prime agents for change, by subverting this very system to leverage the finance to provide new affordable social-housing for all.

Similarly the proposal by international office Plan Común (p. 36) for a giant public greenhouse in Graz, Austria questions the economic drivers behind the development of cities today and the gradual privatisation of public urban spaces – and ways to change this.

The issue of borders, and their breaking down, seems to be a running theme – not least in the idea of the future itself as some bordered off territory observed from afar or indeed in the definition of what being an architect means – but also in the ways architecture and design can impact on new ways of living and interacting. So in Lavinia Scaletti's contribution (p. 194), she explores the breakdown of traditional ideas of the private versus the communal, as a consequence of the new forms of nomadic inner city-living forced on many priced out from permanent accommodation, proposing new structures designed to support – and indeed celebrate – this, a new infrastructure of shared resources and facilities.

Linnea Våglund and Leo Fidjeland (p. 92) in their work question the fundamental division between the manmade and natural, looking at what a future of genetically designed nature – and of architecture and design made from artificial "natural" materials – could be, and how it might shift our relationship to the world around us and our ideas of home.

Meanwhile it is the creative reworking of the tools of narrative and communication in architecture and the tropes of representation that Jana Čulek (p. 156) analyses. She considers how the use of storytelling in the representation of Dutch architecture has been a factor in its success, and looks at how a combination of visual and textual narrative can better explain architecture to its users.

A desire to reframe the "narrative" of architecture also drives the work of Guerilla Architects (p. 134), who seek to recast ideas of public space through playful or subversive actions and interventions – cooking, cleaning and mobile co-working around empty buildings and lots – acts that help question and reimagine the city around us.

Still for all the barrier bending, not least of the old silos of "the profession" of architecture, the core skills and expertise that architects through their training can uniquely bring to issues, remain. This can be clearly seen in the work of Jan Glasmeier and a.gor.a architects (p. 144) on the Thai-Burma border and in Chiang Mai, where their design and construction of education centres for marginalised groups, utilises both established local patterns of building whilst incorporating innovations from their own training and background in Europe.

Their work underlines the constant thread that binds all the work presented here – and that has always underpinned the impulse for good architecture – the hope and optimism for making a better world – even if incrementally, project by project, bit-by-bit.

Rob Wilson
&beyond

No Future

Architectural practice
for the living present

By Matias Echanove
and Rahul Srivastava

No Future

Architectural practice for the living present

By Matias Echanove and Rahul Srivastava

"We are now forced to see our future as something that must be carved out of the present; pragmatically, incrementally and tactically."

Matias Echanove and Rahul Srivastava of the URBZ collective believe the architectural profession needs to stop projecting instrumental, utopian solutions for the future, and engage pragmatically with messy reality as it unfolds – they propose a new way of practice that would be far more radical and optimistic with their call for architects to get tooled-up, get back in the field and get their hands dirty. And they are leading by example.

Seen from Mumbai, an urban agglomeration of about 20 million people, which generates 20 per cent of India's GDP, architecture seems like a nice idea that, along with countless other social ambitions, has found little resonance in the contemporary world.

URBZ

URBZ is an experimental research and action collective founded by Matias Echanove and Rahul Srivastava, with collaborators in Mumbai, Goa, Geneva, New York, Bogotá and São Paulo. Since 2008, URBZ has organised collaborative workshops, conducted field research, generated ideas and projects and produced web content about urban space and places. URBZ believes that residents are experts in their neighbourhoods and develops concepts, tools methodologies that allow architects, urbanists and policymakers to tap into that knowledge pool.

Echanove and Srivastava are also the co-directors of the Institute of Urbanology, which has offices in Mumbai and Goa, India. They have authored numerous essays and commentaries and their work has been exhibited from MoMA in New York to the MAXXI in Rome and the São Paulo Cultural Center.

Matias Echanove studied government and economics at the London School of Economics, urban planning at Columbia University, and urban information systems at the University of Tokyo. Rahul Srivastava studied social and urban anthropology in Mumbai, Delhi and Cambridge, UK.

Previous and this page: Mahatma Gandhi Road in Dharavi, Mumbai is a flood of activities. Photo: Julien Gregorio 2013 © URBZ

Perhaps it is not that architecture doesn't have a future, but rather that the notion of the future itself has become anachronistic. Bruno Latour says we lost the future somewhere in the twentieth century and are now only left with an *avenir*.

Avenir literally means "what is to come". Unlike the future, which we once believed we could construct, *l'avenir* is not something we can anticipate or control. What is coming at us is the by-product of our past projections. Failed socialist and capitalist utopias of the twentieth century have left behind a toxic mix of social injustice and environmental wreckage that we must now deal with.

We have lost faith in a version of the future that would be radically better than the present. The notion of a mechanical and linear future into which we could teleport ourselves has given way to something else. We are now forced to see our future as something that must be carved out of the present; pragmatically, incrementally and tactically. This is not inexorably tragic.

Responding to our present condition and sorting out the mess requires no less creativity than drawing the future on a blank page. But it is a different kind of creativity. The incremental approach takes the present condition, however bad, as the only possible starting point. The pragmatic mindset reminds us that all we can wish for is a better version of what we have already. We can't masterplan our way to a perfect future, but we can recognise the potential hidden in even the most difficult situations and help fulfill it.

In Mumbai, 60 per cent of the population are estimated to be living in slums. This means that they are left to

cope on their own, with quasi-non-existent support from the state, and quasi-ubiquitous repression from mainstream institutions. At the other end of the spectrum, luxurious skyscrapers are mushrooming like there is no tomorrow, following only the irrational logic of real estate speculation. As a result, half a million flats are left vacant in Mumbai, a city where it is not uncommon for a family of eight people to live in a 20 square metre apartment.

A worker overhears his neighbours chatting outside. Back alleys are full of a variety of uses. Homes themselves often double up as work spaces. Photo: Ishan Tankha, June 2014 © URBZ

This landscape of new tall buildings, which mirrors the dated exuberance of twentieth-century New York, Chicago or Hong Kong, seems to function better without architects. Speculative urban development doesn't demand design skill as much as accounting and legal expertise. Many young architects enter the market full of ideas and enthusiasm, but quickly lose hopes and illusions when they realise that what is demanded of them is not actual design but rather translating Excel sheets into buildings.

My home is not a slum: residents welcome you to their home in Dharavi – otherwise misrepresented as the largest slum in Asia. Photo: Brooks Reynolds, June 2010 © URBZ

Given the lack of importance accorded to architecture and design at the high end of the construction spectrum, one would expect that architects would be rushing to where they are most needed: to work in slums, where people struggle with fundamentals like ventilation, light and space optimisation.

But in fact, virtually no architects operate in slums in Mumbai. They are not equipped for it. When architects come to a slum, it is usually to plan what will emerge post eviction. No wonder local residents view them with suspicion.

The way we conceive architecture practice, the tools used and its very language seems totally ill-fitted to address the issues with which most people are confronted in emergent megacities.

Academic institutions in charge of training architects seem to exist in a space-time warp where the future can still be conceived as a total project – architectural, social and political. The same is true of most architectural museums and galleries. These big white boxes only seem to exist to reassure us that there are still stories worth being told; architectural fairy tales that we would love to believe. They show good work for a good world that doesn't exist. Talented architects in Mumbai work almost exclusively on private villas located in the far off periphery, gated and out of sight – shielded from the city's grim reality.

Nothing illustrates the disconnect between architects and the city better than the way houses are actually built in Mumbai's densest neighbourhoods, which are bustling with construction activity. In conventional practice, an architectural drawing is indispensable to translate projects into objects. However, in an adverse context, where occupancy rights are not fully recognised, responsiveness is everything. In such a context, a plan or a drawing serves almost no purpose. Conception and construction happen simultaneously.

The classic architectural plan fails precisely because it is based on the naïve and dangerous belief that you can erase a little bit of the present world and replace it with a piece from the future which will fit right in. But it won't fit in so-called slums because the rules are different. An architect walking in a Mumbai slum is like a "prawn" in the sci-fi film *District 9*; a lost alien, whose power is reduced to zero because nothing corresponds to what he has learned.

Previous page: A fictional street in Dharavi, Mumbai based on architectural ideas provided by artisans in Dharavi. (Ismini Christakopoulou, Jai Bhadgaonkar, Matias Echanove, 2016)

This page: Architectural fantasy for URBZ' *Reclaim Growth* project in 2014, of a high-tech Dharavi where infrastructure propels incremental growth. Render: sP+a © URBZ

If architecture is to survive at all in a world of infinite complexity, where adaptability and reactivity are essential, the practise must be completely reinvented. Parametric urban design will not save us – despite whatever some generation-x prophets may be preaching. Supersizing the architectural objects and adding great internal complexity thanks to supercomputing capacities, will not be enough to respond to challenges that come from outside the practice and outside the project. Gated communities, university campuses, Special Economic Zones and smart cities are neurotic responses to the prevailing feeling among architects and planners that they are losing control.

We reject this gated future and the kind of architectural practice that feeds into it. We don't want to run away from the world, no matter how toxic and unpredictable it is. Instead, we believe that twenty-first century urban practitioners must reinvent their role and invent new modes of engagement with the present reality. We believe that the best starting point is to learn from the existing context at all scales and work with the people who generate it locally.

As practitioners, we must be pragmatic, daring and optimistic. We must learn to deal with emergent forms. This necessarily implies another relationship to one's own creativity. It is not about imposing one order onto another, but about connecting one's own expertise with the knowledge of other actors who are rooted in their immediate reality. ■

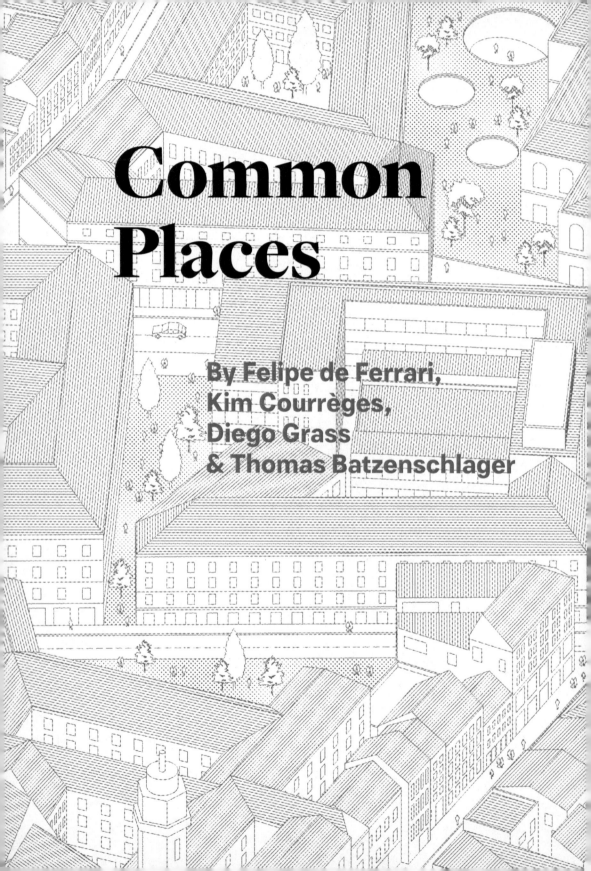

Common Places

By Felipe de Ferrari,
Kim Courrèges,
Diego Grass
& Thomas Batzenschlager

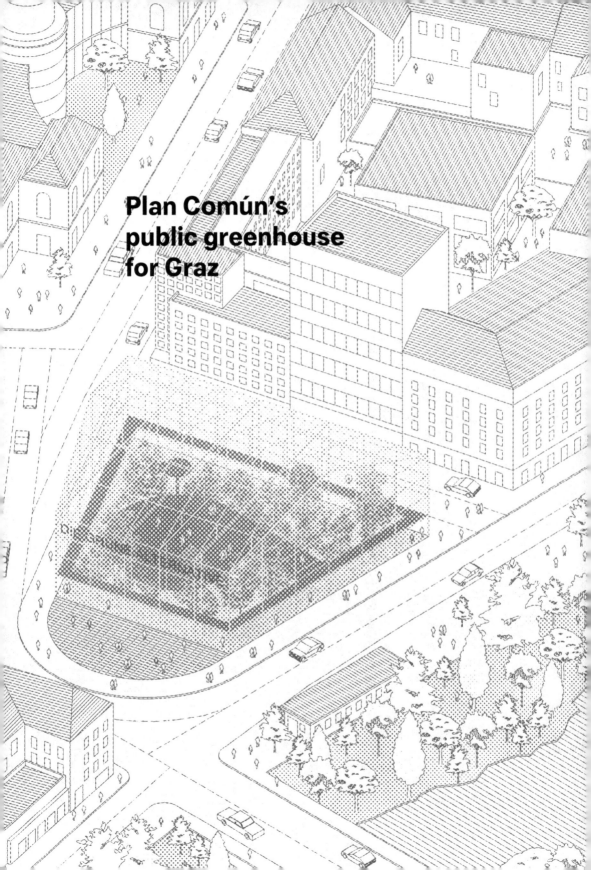

**Plan Común's
public greenhouse
for Graz**

"The goal is to offer alternatives, which reaffirm the public value of architecture as the way of thinking and building our cities."

Common Places

Plan Común's public greenhouse for Graz

By Felipe de Ferrari, Kim Courreges, Diego Grass & Thomas Batzenschlager

Critiquing the economic impulse behind the construction of urban spaces, Chilean office Plan Común take an actively political approach to reclaiming the right to the city with a public greenhouse proposal for Graz in Austria.

Common Places takes a critical position towards what is happening around us.

Common Places draws on the behaviour of people, buildings and things.

Common Places comes out of a critical understanding of specific contexts and programmes.

Common Places has a disregard for the status quo, including commissions and clients.

Common Places proceeds from an active engagement with ordinary demands and needs.

Common Places follows a clear strategy to maximise collective space in every project.

Common Places exhibits an economy of means, a radical understanding of resources such as time.

Regardless of the usual pragmatic aspirations that many of us may have, it is impossible to strip off the ideologies of our cities. In many countries (in our case Chile) we live under a neoliberal model, one in which cities are understood as mere devices to increase the market value of private property.

At the same time, our cities are also victims of the conceptual inability and lack of vision exhibited by local authorities, urban experts and decision-makers. This has provoked the proliferation of indeterminate terrains,

Plan Común

Plan Común has been developing *Common Places* since 2012: strategies to maximise and strengthen public and collective space – understood as a key aspect of architecture, regardless of its scale or programme – using the means of simple architecture tools: critical discourse, research, design and building. We are convinced that radical, basic – even silent – forms are more likely to be relevant and universal, and serve as a support for collective use and imagination. "We use a critical and strategic approach towards briefs and commissions, in order to question and transform spatial hierarchy and uses. We intend to work within an ethic of the collective, aiming at relevance and usefulness for the many."

Previous page: Proposal for a public greenhouse in Andreas-Hofer-Platz in Graz, Austria, 2016. Isometric drawing © Plan Común

the generic (in the pre- and post-Koolhaas sense) and "common" places, in the worst sense of the word.

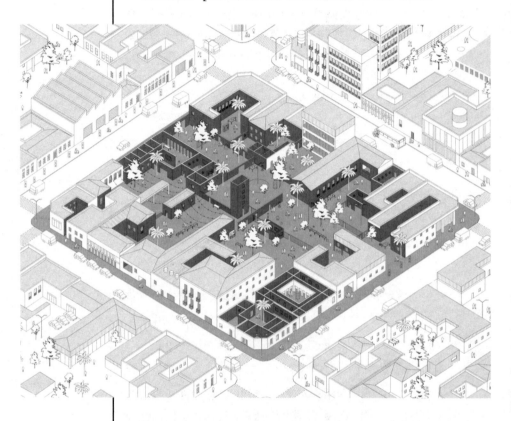

Common Places research: public interiors. © Plan Común

In reaction to this and other related issues, we can see how communities and societies around the world are now mobilising against the consequences and iniquities of the system: recent demonstrations in Chile, Spain, Brazil and the United States are just the tip of the iceberg of reaction against the many inconsistencies within our models of development, distribution of wealth and lifestyles. Citizens are aiming to reclaim the public sphere. This has also been an important stimulus for our practice: we try to engage our work within a framework of radical transformation in opposition to the neoliberal context within which we operate.

As architects, designers, authorities and citizens, we must reclaim our common rights to the public realm in the city. The city is controlled at present by the ups and downs of the market economy. We believe our discipline could counteract this process by creating collective public spaces that hold no value for the market economy – ones that are even sometimes detrimental to private or individual interests – by taking a strategic approach to architecture and thus producing new ways to inhabit the world.

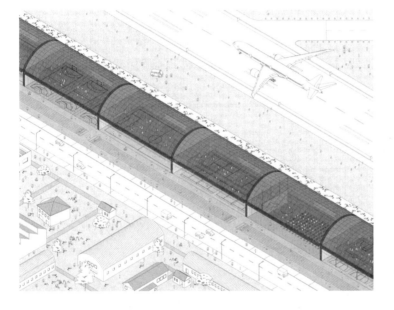

Common Places research: continuous sheds. © Plan Común

Common Places is a collaborative research project initiated and promoted by the Chilean architecture office Plan Común, founded in 2012. Its focus is on research and the production of strategies and projects for maximising public and collective spaces. This began through questioning the validity of current operative models – whether ideological, economic, cultural or normative – in order to produce new and fertile public spaces using our own design skills and architectural tools. The goal

"We propose demercantilised, political and strategic projects for the public and society at large."

is to offer alternatives, which reaffirm the public value of architecture as the way of thinking and building our cities. Within this are all kinds of interesting themes and issues, from the urban to the intimate private scale. The potential of architecture to help generate these spaces is unlocked using disciplinary tools such as text and drawings utilising canonical architectural elements. We propose demercantilised, political and strategic projects for the public and society at large: 50 strategies designed by a network of collaborating architects around the world, that should be activated by a community mobilised to shaping our future cities. The catalogue of strategies, due to be published soon, is just a first phase of the research. We are interested in finding a real context for them and to deal with a real network of actors in order to pursue further the feasibility of each case.

In order to test one of the strategies in a real context, the House of Architecture (HDA) in Graz and ISSS research&architecture, invited Plan Común to propose an alternative transformation of Andreas-Hofer-Platz – a historical plot in the centre of the city – in the context of the *Form follows...* exhibition held at the HDA in 2016.

Context

Originally the site of a Carmelite church and monastery – and known as *Karmeliterplatz* – the earlier buildings were demolished to make way for a fish market. The plot was then sold by the Graz Municipality in 1913 and today contains a subterranean parking garage – one of the most important in the city centre – and a service/bus station. Although the site – now called Andreas-Hofer-Platz – is now private property and not a product of specific urban planning, local citizens continue to call it a "square".

In 2012, a competition was organised by Acoton Real Estate, which bought the site from Shell AG in 2008 for 12.5 million euro. The brief was to build commercial stores, offices, restaurants and housing over the maximum allowable area of 13,500 square metres. At that time the budget for the whole project was 50 million euro and the winning proposal was a design by Atelier Thomas Pucher. For us, the results of the competition were not good enough. Our critique is not just of the design approach taken in the different proposals but mainly of the attitude of the participating architects in the competition. All the proposals we reviewed lacked critical awareness and they all fell short of the demands of the brief. According to the curators of an exhibition at Haus der Architektur (in which this proposal was included), the public demand was for more green space rather than office space. Four years since the competition, the status of the square still remains unclear.

Plan Común saw an architectural counter-proposal as the best way to move on from this stasis. Our proposal therefore is to build a public greenhouse of 2,100 square metres, defined by a double-pitched roof form. The greenhouse responds directly to the demands of Graz citizens, offering a volume of air warmer than outside, the humidity perfect for growing different plants, a pool to collect rainwater from outside and a garden to colonise the plinth and polycarbonate walls of the greenhouse's interior. In its centre, the existing bus station will be updated to allow space for small shops and workshops related to agriculture; its roof will be reinforced and converted into an open terrace for different uses with views towards the garden and surroundings. The existing

Proposal:
Public Greenhouse

Previous page and this page: Interior of the public greenhouse proposed for Andrea-Hofer-Platz, Graz. © Plan Común

subterranean parking could be updated to contain complementary facilities for future stages of the project. This new public "void" provides a unique spatial condition in the context of Graz. It will act as an experimental field to be appropriated by citizens of all ages.

Message: "Die Grüne Alternative"

The political reference of the text on the billboard that forms part of the proposal is straightforward: *Die Grüne Alternative* (The Green Alternative) – the slogan of the Green Party in Austria which has been relatively successful in containing the steady rise of the extreme-right in the country, setting an example – from our perspective – for the rest of the world. Architecture can also contribute towards disrupting the logic of the extreme right in Austria, Europe and abroad and helping counteract its rise.

The slogan: *Die Grüne Alternative* also relates to a different possible future for Andreas-Hofer-Platz: one that is not decided by private interests but oriented towards the public realm and aligned with a more sustainable and simple lifestyle. It will be a specific type of greenhouse designed to behave in an urban context and the third recognisable new intervention along the Mur River, after the Kunsthaus and the Murinsel, albeit one less iconic and more humble than its predecessors.

The façade of the proposed public greenhouse across Andrea-Hofer-Platz. © Plan Común

Why should we abandon our hopes regarding public space? Are we condemned to have residual public spaces defined by the market all the time? We call for all the interested institutions, authorities, civic associations and citizens to recover this plot for the city. ■

The Ingot

A housing solution worth its weight in gold

By Jack Self

The Ingot

A housing solution worth its weight in gold

By Jack Self

"Even hardcore neoliberals recognise that macroeconomic growth depends on low-paid workers living close to their places of work, and maximising their disposable income for increased consumption."

Architect and writer Jack Self sees the potential of the architect to impact meaningful social change in a reconfiguration of the relations between finance and social function – and a gold-plated tower in the centre of London.

Jack Self

Jack Self is an architect and writer based in London. He is Director of the REAL foundation and Editor-in-Chief of the *Real Review*. In 2016, Self co-curated the British Pavilion at the Venice Architecture Biennale.

When volumes of mortgages are traded on the markets, the entity being bought and sold is not strictly speaking property. Rather it is a financial abstraction with no intrinsic worth, whose value is derived from estimating the asset value of the underlying real estate. This is possible because market agents "trust" that the institutions issuing the loans have carried out due diligence in minimising the risk of default. Of course it's not faith alone that permits this; there are diverse regulatory requirements and other means of independently calculating the integrity of the mortgages.

The power of abstracting property loans into revenue streams is namely this: the separation of creditor (investor) and debtor (homeowner) by some managing institution liberates the anonymised occupant from

Previous and this page: still from *Real Estates*, a 5-minute animation made in 2013 of the Ingot project: a gold-plated tower of social housing in the City of London. © Jack Self

certain ethical assessments. The investor has no interest, or say in the aesthetic qualities of the home, its manner of occupancy or the lifestyle of its inhabitants. Their only concern is fiscal: that a given sum be paid throughout a given period. The moral dimension of debt is instead the concern of the financial institution, which like a capitalist Ammut – the Ancient Egyptian demoness of judgement – is charged with weighing the debtor's heart against a feather. The source of agency in the perpetuation of neoliberal power relations is almost exclusively the financial institution. This is what makes the architect so impotent a figure of social change; they do not even negotiate the terms of debt directly with the source of the capital, but through tiers of bankers, developers and other corporate bureaucrats.

"Regaining leverage at this level demands a bypassing of the entire development profession."

In order for architects to exercise the kind of agency required to intervene in this process, they must directly mediate between *end-user* (occupant / client) and *investor* (free market equity) – they must leverage the power of property in such a way as to become both the monetary fixer of debt and its moral evaluator. This vision does not at all correspond with that of the *architect-as-developer*. Quite the contrary, regaining leverage at this level demands a bypassing of the entire development profession – eliminating its greed and monopoly and operating in parallel. This is the image of the *architect-as-financier.* The Ingot, a project for a tower in the City of London, might be considered a first attempt at this prospective "derivative architecture", characterised by a total separation between financial form and social function.

The specific goal of the Ingot project was to find a way to make high quality, generously-sized apartments affordable for living-wage workers in or close to the City of London.

Regardless of where on the political spectrum one sits, this is a desirable ambition – even hardcore neoliberals recognise that macroeconomic growth depends on low-paid workers living close to their places of work and maximising their disposable income for increased consumption. A site was selected adjacent to London Bridge, directly on top of the ruins of the ancient Roman forum.

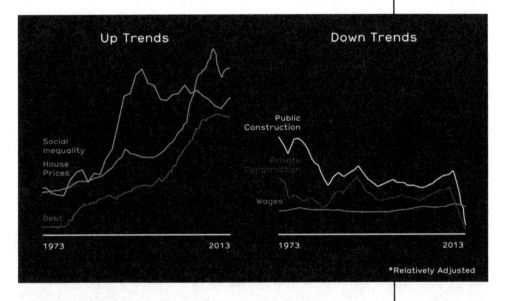

Still from *Real Estates,* 2013.
© Jack Self

Subversion of a system first requires mastering an understanding of how it works. For this reason the starting point had to be an imitation of how a standard developer would approach the project: by conducting a *surplus land value assessment* to determine the potential profit on a building at market rate. This process is not so dissimilar to calculating the surplus equity in a normal home – add up all the costs (price of the land, demolition and construction) then subtract this from the maximum value of a potential structure. Unless developers can extract 20 per cent profit, they rarely bother and sites go undeveloped.

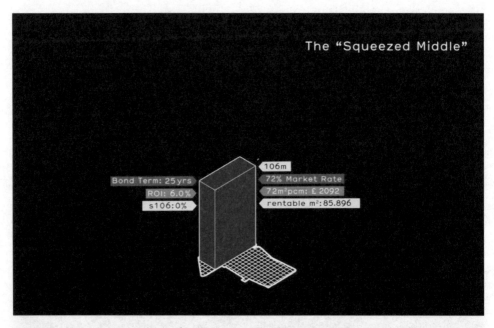

The "Squeezed Middle"

Bond Term: 25 yrs
ROI: 6.0%
s106: 0%

106m
72% Market Rate
72m²pcm: £ 2092
rentable m²: 85.896

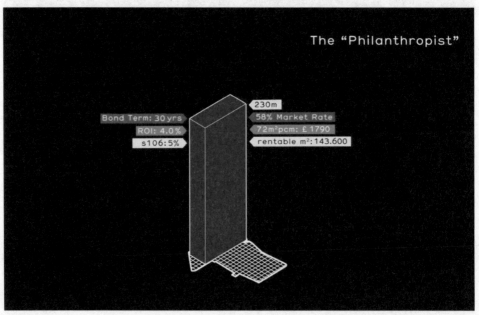

The "Philanthropist"

Bond Term: 30 yrs
ROI: 4.0%
s106: 5%

230m
58% Market Rate
72m²pcm: £ 1790
rentable m²: 143.600

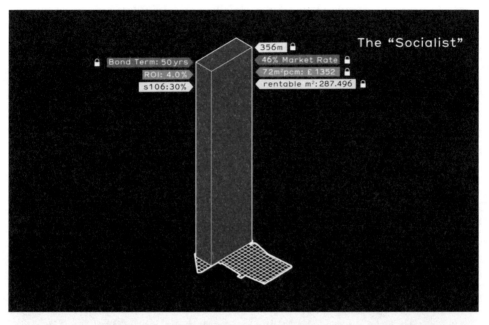

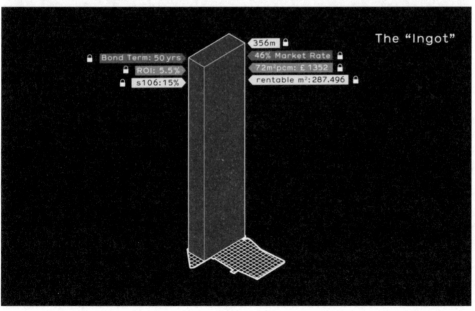

Property development is a constant negotiation between three critical factors: time, space and money – to get closer to the required profit figure developers are always working towards the highest feasible density at the lowest possible cost in the shortest turnaround. The result of the land assessment showed that a 20 per cent profit margin was achievable, making the land viable for standard redevelopment. There was a major problem with this however: no fiddling of the factors could reduce the purchase price very much below market rates – the developer's profit precluded it – making it too expensive for workers on the living wage (who lack equity to buy in any case).

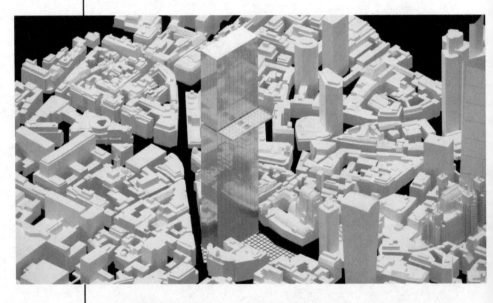

Previous, this page and opposite: Stills from *Real Estates*, 2013. © Jack Self

In order to make an impact on end price, a parametric algorithm was developed to manipulate these factors individually. One important financial precedent for the algorithm was how universities raise equity for constructing new buildings (specifically at UC Berkeley and Queens' College, Cambridge). These institutions issue long-term bonds – often 50 years or longer – to fund new student rooms or science blocks, while the interest on the bond is secured against future tuition. The university ends up paying quite a lot for the investment capital, but does so over such a long period that the repayments are manageable. Schemes like this are highly attractive to entities looking for stable and predictable returns, and investors often include insurers, banks and sovereign or pension funds. If we replace tuition with rent and student rooms with housing, the basic model holds and the developer as a source of finance becomes unnecessary.

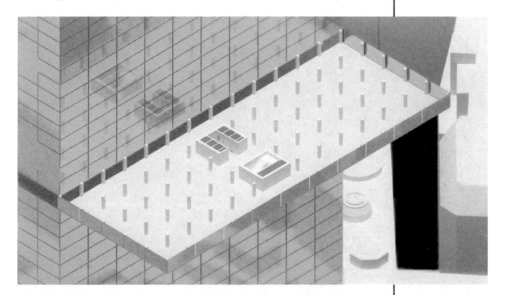

Of course, in theory almost any company can issue a long-term bond – in practice, the rate of interest on such a bond is relative to the trust the markets have in that company. A well-respected international university has leverage where an architect certainly does not. To address this trust issue, the building itself becomes the security underwriting the bond, which can be sold at market rate if at some point the mechanism fails. The market wager then becomes whether the architect is capable of delivering the building on time and to budget.

Security also lies in the fact that if this architect-bank were providing apartments at 46 per cent of the market rate (which is what would be necessary to make it affordable for the living-wage worker) there would have to be a 54 per cent drop in London property prices before it would become unfeasible. The worst housing slump in British history (1914–22) was caused by a combination of the First World War and the introduction of industrial manufacturing techniques in construction (oversupply in the markets), which saw prices fall by around 35 per cent. Given the current climate of unprecedented shortage, probably only a cataclysmic environmental disaster could produce such an effect. To insure against this event, we can also add security into the material of the building itself.

"In a worse case scenario, the Ingot itself is a fungible commodity, a hedged bet against crisis, functioning outside the property market."

There is a direct correlation between economic instability and global gold prices, because of its perceived international fungibility – the acceptance that the equivalent value of a given amount of gold can be mutually substituted with that of other materials. The Ingot's facade would be electroplated with some 170kg of gold. In a worse case scenario, the Ingot itself therefore becomes a fungible commodity, a hedged bet against crisis, functioning outside the property market.

In order for the Ingot to be funded by a 50-year bond, a number of parameters have to be true. The building certainly cannot be sold within the period of the bond, which means inhabitants must accept the idea of never owning the property, but nonetheless retaining usufructuary rights – having rights to enjoy and profit from the property but not to damage or destroy it. To amortise – or pay off – the debt at the bond's maturity, the annual payment (interest plus two per cent of the principal) must be equal to or less than the income gained from rental. In other words, there is a fixed ratio between construction cost and rental revenue that will determine what the annual surplus from a living-wage apartment would be, in turn dictating the massing of the building and its total rentable space. Since the debt is issued and held by a company also responsible for the construction, maintenance, letting and management of the building, the company itself is the location of the moral dimension of the debt obligation (thereby liberating the renter). Needless to say, there are several more complex interrelations in this calculation.

Resolving these parameters required working backwards – starting at the face value of the bond and thereby determining the rate of return. This figure was estimated at 4.5 per cent per annum, which included 2.5 per cent in interest and two per cent in principal repayment. For comparison, over the last century the mean capital gain on a property was just 2.4 per cent per annum. The interest dictated how much surplus an apartment had to generate in rent each year, which fed backwards into how big it could be or how much it could cost per square metre.

This in a nutshell is how the optimised form and volume of the Ingot was arrived at and how it redeploys commonplace financial mechanisms to achieve its specific goal. It has been described as form following finance, although it might be more accurate to say that it is function following finance, where the form is not intrinsically relevant.

This is just one scenario of one particular model, motivated by what I see as a general poverty of aspiration in architecture today – a reluctance to position the

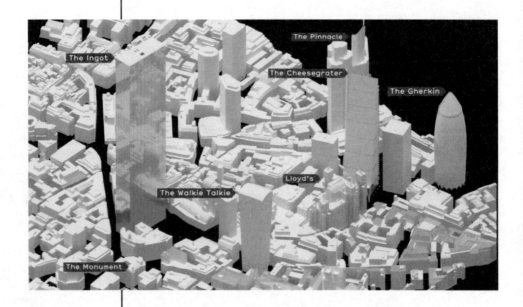

architect as a figure capable of meaningful social change – as well as a lack of pragmatism: inasmuch as our utopian vision for urban x surpasses our actual political influence and economic power. If architecture is to exist as anything more than the ornamental resolution of façades or the sculptural expression of domesticity, it must clearly articulate a new position with regard to the role of property and ownership in the global economy. ■

A Self-Constructed Paradigm

Housing that is about more than just houses

By Sara Neves and Filipe Estrela

A Self-Constructed Paradigm
Housing that is about more than just houses

By Sara Neves and Filipe Estrela

"Gharaunda aims to create conditions to encourage the young to stay in rural areas by choice, with dignity and pride in a rural identity."

Filipe Estrela and Sara Neves describe how, by working together with villagers in rural Bihar, India, they developed a flexible housing model to improve living conditions, in a project that considers the whole building lifecycle – not just the final built form.

We believe that by taking the rural as a valid alternative to the urban, we let cities breathe and contribute to the emancipation of the urban and its transformation.

Gharaunda is an ongoing housing project for low-income families in rural Bihar, India.

The majority of housing projects are focused on the future of cities and the problems coming from their population growth. But does everyone want to live in cities?

India needs about 20 million urban houses and 45 million rural ones. Bihar is the third most populous state in India where 89 per cent live in rural areas and 30 per cent live on less than one euro per day. 50 per cent of their houses

Sara Neves and Filipe Estrela

Architects Sara Neves and Filipe Estrela are graduates of the Faculty of Architecture of the University of Porto (FAUP). They both worked on a number of projects and for several studios until setting up their own independent practice in 2015. They are moved by the same interest in long-term immersive projects and hands-on fieldwork, in which architecture is not the only object or goal.

Previous page: new flexible housing model developed by Sara Neves and Filipe Estrela in Bihar, India.

This page: new housing model seen beyond a typical traditional house. © Sara Neves and Filipe Estrela

A practical approach

are made of raw thatch, bamboo and/or mud, 62 per cent of which have no toilet and 89 per cent of which have no electricity or solar energy.

The young seeking employment in cities suffer difficult living conditions and the pressure on farmland for fast-paced urban growth is leaving behind a trail of destruction in villages, leading to a loss of livelihoods and lack of housing and access to basic services.

45 per cent of Bihar's population are under 20 years old and many of the young would prefer to stay in their villages if they could have access to better living conditions.

So we looked to help reframe these conditions.

The Gharaunda project is focused on rural development through sustainable housing construction. Tailored for the local culture but improving the local standard minimum living requirements, Gharaunda aims to create conditions to encourage the young to stay in rural areas by choice, with dignity and pride in a rural identity.

A new model

In rural Bihar, a *pucca* house, which is a permanent building made with materials resistant to the local weather conditions, is generally the desirable upgrade from the typical *kaccha* house – a building made of basic raw materials that needs to be rebuilt every season. However, even most pucca houses of low-income families don't have a water supply, sewage or even a toilet, and are built with very unstable construction methods that lack foundations.

So we set out to design a new model of housing that achieved a balance between tradition and change.

Our prototype design is not for a specific family, but for several families with different sizes and routines – given the number of people living in the same house can range from two to 21 people. So the house is adaptable to differing family dynamics with customisable rooms.

The interior spaces of the new housing model balance flexibility and privacy. © Sara Neves and Filipe Estrela

The rooms are designed to be completely flexible allowing a family to use them as they see fit: two bedrooms, or four smaller bedrooms, or one bedroom and one living room, or two smaller bedrooms, a smaller living room and a store room. There are two doors to each room meaning a partition – such as a curtain – can be placed in the middle, so that each room – even if divided in four – can be accessed independently.

A large part of the prototype's structure is dedicated to outdoor spaces. In line with tradition, there are two separate verandahs, one for women – facing the courtyard – and one

for men – open to the public space or street. However, the women's verandah is also placed adjacent to the street, separated from the men's verandah by a perforated wall, encouraging communication and reducing the separation between genders.

Previous and this page: Men's verandah adjacent to the street is here joined to the women's *verandah*, separated only by a perforated wall. © Sara Neves and Filipe Estrela

For cooking there seems to be a move to adopt more modern methods over traditional ones, such as cooking in earthen stoves outside and eating on the floor. So while the kitchen space is designed as an indoor standing one, we have connected it with the main verandah to preserve the link with tradition.

Despite efforts to end public defecation, the government has found resistance to change, given local prejudice about having a toilet inside the house. While the villagers requested an indoor bathroom, they preferred one that maintained privacy in its use, separated from the rest of the house. The bathroom opens to the back of the house, only accessible from the outside. Although included in the core structure, it is separate from the life of the rest of the house.

Solid and permanent

Gharaunda takes local materials and techniques as the basis to co-develop and disseminate more advanced construction techniques that incorporate foundations, more robust materials and safer working methods. Bamboo is commonly used locally, as a material it is very resistant and can last for several decades, while its flexibility and bending strength make it an ideal seismic-resistant construction material.

Local materials are used for the construction: bamboo and bricks moulded from the soil-waste of the site. © Sara Neves and Filipe Estrela

Bricks, cast with holes through them, are highly advantageous for several reasons: made from the soil-waste on the construction site which has been excavated for the foundations, these bricks mitigate the need to build double walls, being laid on end in a "rat-trap" bond system that provides good thermal insulation, while allowing for infrastructure to run inside the bricks and providing a neat wall finish.

Infrastructure

The water supply employs a low-cost system, that does not require electricity, providing tap water inside the house. It combines a manual hand-pump, positioned using local techniques, a tank and a network of pipes.

The sewage system employs a local septic system, eco-friendly and affordable. The digested waste can be used as soil-conditioner for agricultural purposes or as biogas fuel.

Electricity meanwhile is provided through a straightforward system that combines all the gadgets onto one simple circuit board, positioning one board in each room.

Spatially the Gharaunda housing model invites in light and natural ventilation.
© Sara Neves and Filipe Estrela

Spatially, the form of Gharaunda also invites in sunlight, encourages natural ventilation and aims to offer beauty and a pleasing atmosphere – because being proud of and enjoying one's house has to be part of minimum living requirements everywhere.

Gharaunda is a tailor-made housing paradigm designed
with the whole lifecycle of a building in mind – from
the diagnosis of the need and the design concept, to its
construction and the businesses involved, their labour
conditions, sales and maintenance – creating new
livelihoods for some in the process and aiming to have a
long-term impact on villagers' lives.

The paradigm

From harnessing the local value chain and its natural
resources, Gharaunda proposes a sustainable housing
model that is almost 100 per cent constructed using local
renewable materials, widely available throughout India.
This allows a potential role as a wider model for rural
development, through its lower budget and ecological
balance. Inspired by local techniques, it is modular,
designed in order to simplify most construction processes,
and to help launch construction businesses at a village
level to produce and build locally, independently of
globalised and centralised systems of production.

Self-constructed paradigms are a demand for architecture
in which processes and form carry equal weight, an
awareness that housing is not just about houses. A housing
paradigm has to take into account more than just the final
product and its end-users: building a house is about jobs
and their conditions, the workers involved and their skills,
resources and their source and who owns them, about
costs and profit, the environment, its protection, and
about waste. The form should embody all these processes
in its development.

*Self-constructed
paradigms*

This project is about shared responsibility based on
interdisciplinarity; moving beyond just the overlap of
specialised domains and based on community immersion
and co-creating with the inhabitants. It is about hands-on

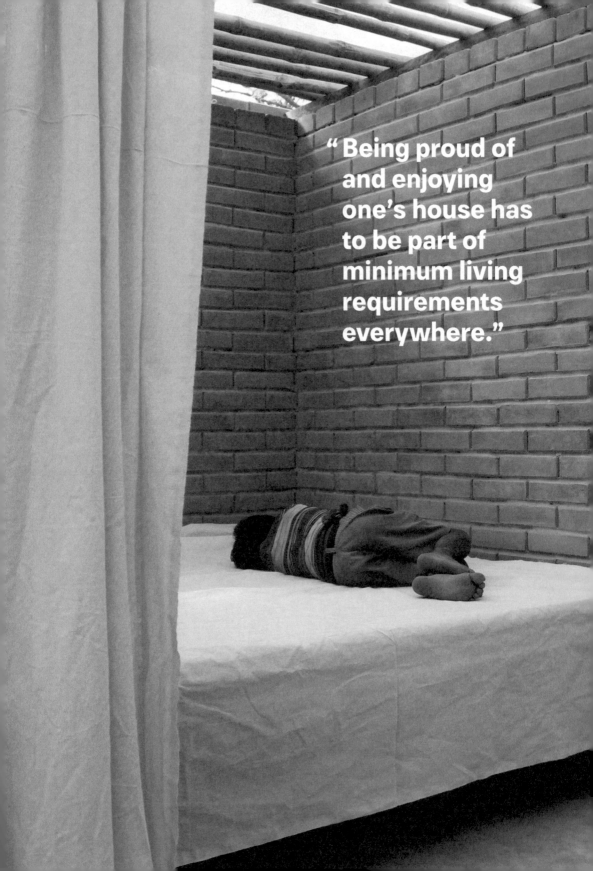

"Being proud of and enjoying one's house has to be part of minimum living requirements everywhere."

Previous page: Housing that prioritises use value not market value; protection not financial security. © Sara Neves and Filipe Estrela

co-building and giving the users the tools to continuously update in response to changing needs.

We need to generate more housing from usable, safe and beautiful forms and building paradigms in which these values are the right of all. The priorities should be: use value not market value; protection not financial security and harmony not brand trend. ■

Biosynthetic Futures

**Speculating on
designing nature
and design as nature**

**By Linnea Våglund
and Leo Fidjeland**

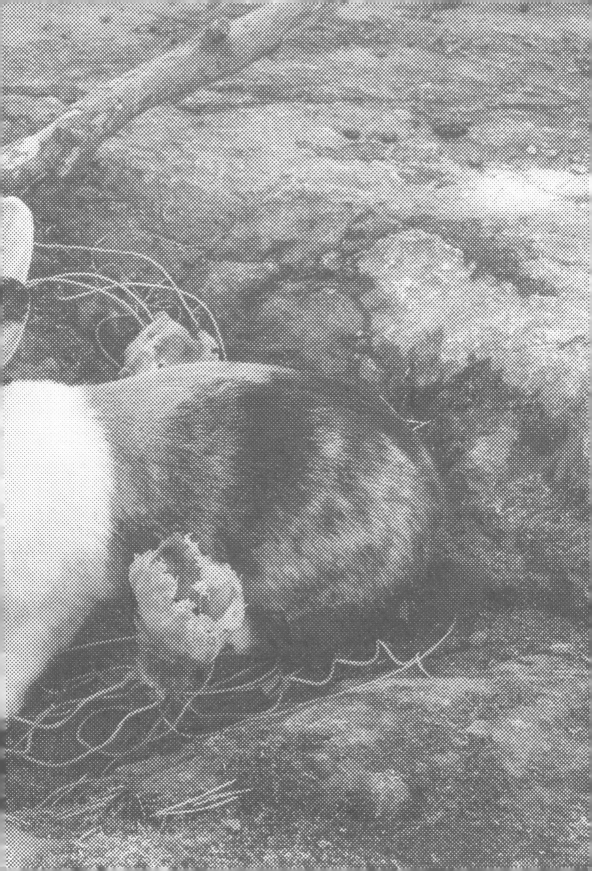

Biosynthetic Futures
Speculating on designing nature and design as nature

By Linnea Våglund and Leo Fidjeland

"We find it very important that the discussion on what to do with the power of synthetic biology is in the hands of citizens and not just scientists and experts with knowledge in the field."

Linnea Våglund and Leo Fidjeland present a series of speculative projects designed to explore how the future of genetically designed nature and design made from artificial "natural" materials could change our relationship with the natural world.

With the emergence of synthetic biology, the foundations of life itself could be subject to major changes. This research area, that combines engineering and the natural sciences, has the goal of creating new biological functions that do not exist naturally. We can now grow meat in laboratories, modify bacteria to produce biomaterials, like spider-silk and cotton, and alter organisms to glow in different colours. We are heading towards a future where we might be able to change organisms however we want – and create new ones.

How will we use this new power? How will it affect us and our relationship with nature? In these projects, current advances are extrapolated into extreme scenarios through the use of speculative design, a type of design meant to facilitate discussion, rather than to solve problems. The scenarios are not a prediction or a forecast of the future, but an imagination of a parallel world, a possible future.

From these futures, speculative artefacts and organisms are designed, materialised and extracted to interact with the public, thereby immersing them in this alternate reality. The discussion of how we should react to this emerging technology is in the hands of the spectator.

Linnea Våglund

Linnea Våglund is a designer focusing on speculative design and science. She has a BFA in Industrial design from Konstfack, University College of Arts, Crafts and Design in Stockholm and is currently studying MA Material Futures at Central Saint Martins in London.

Leo Fidjeland

Leo Fidjeland is a technologist focusing on speculative design and science. He has a BSc in Engineering Physics from the Royal Institute of Technology in Stockholm and is currently studying MA Material Futures at Central Saint Martins in London.

This project has partly been conducted at the Interactive Institute Swedish ICT.

Previous page: Rabbit enjoying the euphonic audible flora. © Annie Åkerman

Audible Flora

A group of DIY bio-hackers design a new sensor plant that detects pollution levels and indicates the result through sound, in order to raise awareness of the worsening environmental situation to their fellow citizens. When the plants are put in beneficial, clean surroundings, they *sing* beautifully. When put in a heavily polluted place, they *scream* a disturbing noise.

Drinking plant nectar to replenish strength. © Annie Åkerman

Initially, the environment is improved due to people responding to these audible, emotional cues of the plants. However, having found a new niche in which to prosper, the plants eventually mutate and spread without control, rendering polluted areas uninhabitable through noise. It's as if nature suddenly has the power to express itself, claiming the right to exist free from pollution.

The Anthropocene, the proposed human geological epoch, heralds mass extinction and loss of biodiversity. But with synthetic biology, we could end up in a state with even more species than before. In a future where parts (or all) of nature have been designed by humans, what would biodiversity mean? Could human-designed plants even be considered natural?

Audible Flora has been designed with a good intentions: to improve the environment and reduce pollution. But with the power to quickly change organisms, there is a risk that sensitive ecosystems that have taken thousands of years to develop are disrupted. When do we classify a species as invasive – when plants created in laboratories are not native to any location? What is the moral difference between natural adaptation and human design?

Imagine a future where corporations and governments control what species that exist. Would they care about genetic pollution, when they today often don't even care about particle pollution?

In the year 2030, on the brink of ecological collapse, when overconsumption threatens human existence, factories are hastily shut down to give some breathing room to the planet.

Biosynthetic Possessions

To reconcile our lifestyle with the ecosystem, only biological and digital goods are allowed on the market. This leads to a global surge in synthetic biology research, and soon, we can modify organisms to grow into any shape or function: matching the products of the old world.

A table can now be grown from a genetically modified seed. It requires care and attention to live and prosper, but in return, it repairs itself and can multiply and spread.

"I'm helping my neighbour to water her table while she is on vacation". © Annie Åkerman

The teddy bear that your child once treated as if it was alive, now is. Growing with the child, getting bigger as the child gets older. Bioluminescent fungi replace lamps given the lack of electricity.

Back in the present, GM crops are already being patented, transforming a species into intellectual property and a commodity. In this future scenario, nature is being transformed into a possession and our possessions are a part of nature. When the border between nature and product dissolves, how will our relation to our surroundings change?

If your products were alive, would you value them differently? Would it ease some of the most unsustainable aspects of our consumer lifestyle? Or would the mindset travel in the opposite direction, with nature being regarded as something that could easily be replaced and recreated, thus losing its value. Would we develop the same estranged relationship towards nature that we have with products today?

In the face of bee extinction, an alluring plant that taps into human desires and needs has started appearing around outdoor gyms. The passing humans drink the plant nectar to replenish their strength. Some pollen sticks in their shirt, and as they drink from the next plant, the vital cross-pollination occurs. Nobody really knows if the plants appeared by a random mutation or if they were given a "helping hand" by local bio-hackers.

Human Beeings

In a world where we see plants as products, plants might see us as consumers – just as in Human Beeings, where a plant has survived bee extinction by adapting to human health norms. In such a future, would only the plants that tended to human desires and needs thrive in this new "market"? Do we only care about something if it adds value to the human condition? Or does untouched nature have a value in its own right?

All species transform their surroundings and in that sense change ecological and environmental conditions. What makes the human transformation of the planet remarkable is the speed with which it is occurring, and the fact that it is (at least in part) driven by conscious agency.

Closing Thoughts

The job of speculative design is to show that things could in fact be very different. To make people believe that change is possible and that we have a chance to alter our values, norms, societies and lives.

Audible flora rendering
polluted areas uninhabitable
by noise. © Annie Åkerman

We find it very important that the discussion on what to
do with the power of synthetic biology is in the hands of
citizens and not just scientists and experts with knowledge
in the field. As designers, we can be catalysts to such
discussions by conceptualising, materialising and
visualising possible futures. A materialisation believable
enough to stimulate the same discussion as that if the
scenarios were real. ■

Behind the Front

Rethinking urban waterways beyond pretty views and high prices

By Manon Mollard

Behind the Front

Rethinking urban waterways beyond pretty views and high prices

By Manon Mollard

"Could we rediscover waterways as sites of production, of fundamental use and value to our cities – rather than solely as places of leisure and entertainment?"

Manon Mollard

Manon Mollard is an
architectural designer and
writer. Born in France and
raised between Europe
and Latin America, she has
worked in Colombia and is
currently based in London,
where she is features editor
at the Architectural Review.

Previous page: At street
level an illusory situation of
emergency creates a flood,
converting transient qualities
into mirages. © Manon
Mollard

This page: Below ground,
volumes act like sponges:
absorbing, temporarily
holding and eventually
releasing water. © Manon
Mollard

The architectural designer and writer Manon Mollard issues a call to "reverse engineer" urban waterways and harness the flows of water that keep the city serviced and dry by rethinking its infrastructure of fresh water, rain run-off and sewage.

Familiar fragments of London appear below the pavement – green spaces, literally pushed down, become underground gardens while façade reflections, transferred down, offer fleeting glimpses of daily life. © Manon Mollard

A few years ago, a developer working on a housing proposal in central London realised that if he built a canal through the middle of the scheme, and brought with it moorings and boats and all the things that people like about canalside living, the whole cost of actually building that canal would be more than covered by the increase in the prices he could now charge for the flats adjacent to it.

"Waterfront living" is trendy, exclusive and mostly about paying for a nicely framed view out of one's window – floor-to-ceiling glazed openings that take full advantage of the watery vistas being an imperative. Currently under construction in London, the Nine Elms Regeneration site, for example, feels like the apogee of this lifestyle so cherished by property speculators. It is Britain's biggest housing development – a fact – but the project website's claim that it is "the greatest transformational story at the heart of the world's greatest city" is much more questionable. Stretching from Battersea Park to Lambeth Bridge, the project is remodelling a staggering three kilometre stretch along the Thames into a sparkling new district complete with green spaces, cultural amenities and luxury apartments awaiting to be splurged on by future homeowners – even if the vast majority of these are likely to be foreign investors too busy to drop their suitcases in London and enjoy their newly bought, very own river views.

When water isn't there to be picture-framed, it tends to be encased in gigantic tunnels running underneath our cities. If romantic views of sunsets over riverbanks are at one end of the spectrum, at the other there are the rivers of everyday raw sewage and waste water from homes and businesses. The latest tunnel to date is Thames Tideway, the construction of which started at the beginning of 2016. Known as London's "Super Sewer", it is the biggest infrastructure project ever undertaken by the UK water industry – also a fact – but the claim on the project

"We need to rethink our systems and reinvest our waterways with meaning."

"Rather than just hiding this resource away, could it not also be used in making a great piece of city?"

website that it is "world-leading British engineering at its best", promising to "deliver a lasting legacy for London", is also much more questionable. Designed to stop the 39 million tonnes of sewage overflow that end up in the river each year, the Super Sewer proposal might buy a bit of time, but merely postpones the need for a real solution to the problem. How long until we need yet another bigger, deeper tunnel to absorb the future overflow?

Admittedly, waterways haven't brought out the best from the architectural community in the recent years. The reality is that architects just don't seem to get involved. When talking about urban waterways, decisions are handed over to engineers and property speculators. Is it because of the scale – too large? Is it because of the programme – too dirty? Is it too demeaning a field for a profession that aspires to more sophisticated projects?

Not so long ago, waterways played a true civic role in the planning of the city, helping generate architecture that was significant. In the eighteenth and nineteenth centuries, the Strand, the street running along one of the most important stretches of the Thames in central London, was a place of real social invention and exploration in the modernising metropolis. Joseph Bazalgette, the great nineteenth century civil engineer laid the Northern Outfall Sewer under it, one of the first stretches of the Circle Line Underground route was dug beneath it, and alongside it the Adam Brothers designed the Adelphi Buildings, which marked the birth of the *terrace* as a type – which went on to become the most important housing idea of the late eighteenth and early nineteenth centuries in England.

Undoubtedly, waterways don't play the same commercial, social or industrial role they used to, yet our need for

When cities are landscape and interiors are public, new types of spaces can emerge and visitors are invited to explore wet gabion corridors. © Manon Mollard

infrastructure is greater than ever. Water is clearly vital to the future of the planet and the future of our cities for environmental reasons – global warming and flooding – but also because waterways, bereft of their previous uses, are now left void. No one speaks for them and we are letting them become sources of spectacle at best – deep socio-political boundaries at worst. Downriver from the waterfront living vistas, the Thames is still used to transport waste and aggregates. Could we rediscover

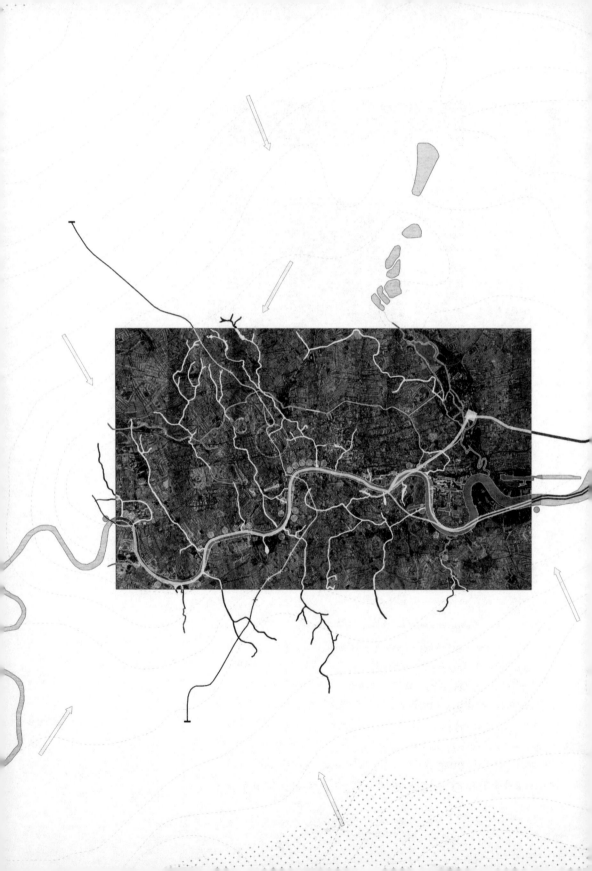

waterways as sites of production, of fundamental use and value to our cities – rather than solely as places of leisure and entertainment?

Two thirds of London's rivers are currently buried underground in 2,000 miles of brick tunnels, channelled into underground culverts as invisible carriers of waste. Today it seems the Industrial Age's spirit of civic innovation has been lost and the same tired models keep re-appearing. The logic and the numbers backing the Super Sewer project just don't add up. Surface runoff from rain, for example, constitutes a rich source of potential, a base material to be worked with.

We need to rethink our systems and reinvest our waterways with meaning. Rather than pushing infrastructure to the outskirts and enclosing flows of water into kilometres of pipes flowing underneath our buildings, we should insert it into the core. It is a process of reverse evolution, one that challenges the role of infrastructure in our cities. We should make room for water by preparing spaces to absorb excesses of storm water, effectively flooding entire pieces of city when needed. This new form of infrastructure in turn would generate true urban interiors. Vertical landscapes and narratives are created, the ground floor gains in thickness and the street level is no longer the only datum. Connections between levels are maintained, either physically or simply visually. Plays of water, light and reflections are orchestrated to create new relationship between the city's different layers, echoing past stories. ■

Opposite: London's culverted rivers flowing into the Thames constitute some of the city's incredible network of underground structures. © Manon Mollard

Weaponised Architecture

Deconstructing the logic of architectural violence

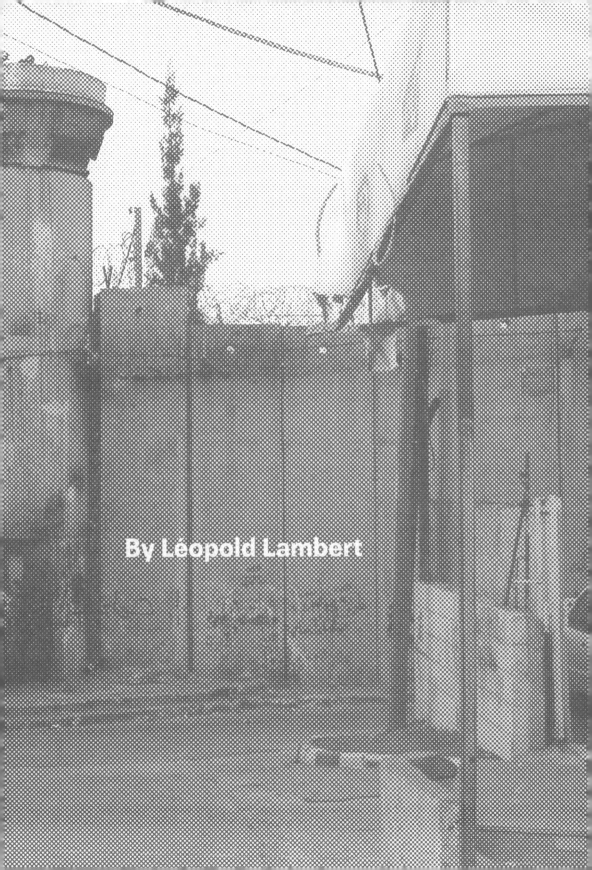

By Leopold Lambert

Weaponized Architecture
Deconstructing the logic of architectural violence

By Léopold Lambert

"The determination of who designs/builds architecture and benefits from the control of its violence on bodies has necessarily drastic political consequences."

From bus shelters to borders, the spatial consequences of political agendas are impossible to escape: Léopold Lambert breaks down the violence inherent in our built environment and encourages the profession towards more active acknowledgement and resistance in the field.

What does it mean to say that architecture is a political weapon? In order to answer this question, we need to see how architecture is, firstly, a weapon (that is, how architecture has a propensity for violence) and secondly, how such a propensity is necessarily instrumentalised by one or several political agendas.

Let's begin with some non-anthropocentric considerations. The material assemblage we call a wall and the material assemblage we call a body are both situated spatially in the world at a particular moment. Because of their material properties, none of these two assemblages (nor any other) can occupy the same spatial coordinates at the same time. What this means is that in order for a body to occupy the same spatial coordinates as a wall – a requirement if this body wants to *cross* the wall – a shock will occur, detrimental to both assemblages; this shock is what we call violence.

The first political dimension through which we can think of this encounter between the *wall* and the *body* lies in the fact that walls are almost always built in such a way that the body's core energy (i.e. without the use of tools) is incapable of affecting their structural integrity. This determines the conditions of the encounter: although the violence will be reciprocal, the degree of violence will not be symmetrical. In other words, the violence deployed by the wall on the body will be much greater than the one deployed by the body on the wall.

Léopold Lambert

Léopold Lambert is the founder and editor-in-chief of *The Funambulist*, a bimestrial printed and digital magazine associated with two open-access online platforms: a blog and a podcast. His work is dedicated to the formulation of questions about the political relationships between the designed/built environment and bodies. His main fields of involvement are in Palestine, the Paris *banlieues*, and "Fortress Europe". He is the author of *Weaponized Architecture: The Impossibility of Innocence* (dpr-barcelona, 2012), *Topie Impitoyable: The Corporeal Politics of the Cloth, the Wall, and the Street* (punctum books, 2016), and *La politique du bulldozer: la ruine palestinienne comme projet israélien* (B2, 2016).

Previous page: The Apartheid Wall in East-Jerusalem, 2015. © Léopold Lambert

The consequence of such an asymmetrical spread of power is the ability for architecture to organise bodies in space, as much through the violence described above, as through its potentiality, usually internalised by bodies – we, as bodies, do not need to encounter a wall to know that we will have trouble crossing it. We can already see how this essential organising, and by extension controlling, function of architecture appeals to political agendas. Surrounding a body with walls enforces the incarceration of this body. Of course, the invention of the wall was quickly followed by the invention of a mechanism to mitigate the potential violence described above: the door, allowing the porosity of a wall to be moderated by making a small part of it rotate at will. But here again, the door was not invented alone; it came with a lock and an associated key that allows only certain bodies to transform the impermeable wall into a punctually porous one.

"Architecture creates processes of inclusion and exclusion of bodies that either reinforce or create unequal social conditions."

Whether the key holder is the agent benefiting from private property legislation, the warden of a prison, or an apartheid state, the determination of who designs/builds architecture and benefits from the control of its violence on bodies has necessarily drastic political consequences. Even the seemingly innocent shelter or bus stop in the pouring rain illustrates the relationships of power that are created through architecture. Should this shelter become filled with bodies seeking architecture's protection against the rain, the snow, or anything else, additional bodies will be excluded from such protection. Whether the rule "first come, first served" is ethically legitimate or not is not (yet) the problem here: what is important to observe is that architecture creates processes of inclusion and exclusion of bodies that either reinforce or create unequal social conditions.

Given these intrinsic political effects, and acknowledging the necessity to engage with architecture rather than giving up on it, we therefore need to examine what these effects are directed against in a given society. Almost always, partially because the drastic political consequences of architecture are either ignored or denied, these effects are directed in such a way that they reinforce the state-driven and/or normative relationships of power between bodies. Architectural projects motivated explicitly with such political programmes are, of course, the easiest to describe in this matter. The apartheid territorial and architectural apparatuses designed and built by the Israeli government and army in Palestine may be the most tragically illustrative examples of such deliberateness.

Portion of the border wall built by the Viktor Orbán administration between Hungary and Serbia, 2015. © Léopold Lambert

The infamous wall that separates the main part of
the West Bank from the rest of Palestine, built at the
beginning of the twenty-first century under the Ariel
Sharon administration, is of course, the most expressive
use of architecture to implement the state of apartheid.
However, many other architectural forms also contribute
to it: the blockade of the 1.8 million of Palestinians living
in Gaza, the 139 Israeli civil settlements in the West Bank
and East Jerusalem and their neighbouring military bases,
the segregated infrastructure (roads, water, electricity, the
internet, etc.), the numerous temporary and permanent
military checkpoints that regulate / prevent Palestinian
movement between cities, not to forget the walls built on
the borders of historical Palestine, preventing the return
of five million refugees in Lebanon, Syria, and Jordan.

Container refugee camp of
Calais so-called *Jungle*, 2016.
© Léopold Lambert

The logic of the architectural violence at work in Palestine
is nevertheless not confined to this territory. We find
its avatars in contemporary Europe, between states of
emergency (in France and Belgium for instance) that
transform cities' public space and the specific measures

taken to deny proper hospitality to hundreds of thousands of bodies fleeing their countries because of military and/ or economic violence. Border walls, container camps, detention centres, fortified police stations, fences, checkpoints, the numerous architectural apparatuses that are flourishing in the European Union and its periphery, although not all targeting the same bodies, have in common the myth of a homogenous national identity epitomised by a neocolonial structural racism.

We would be mistaken, however, to think of the violence of these political programmes as exceptional or responding only to the particular drama of current events. The way most cities are territorially organised enforces a social segregation between populations that are economically and racially categorised. The example of Paris is particularly illustrative here. Its *banlieues* (suburbs), where 80 per cent of its inhabitants live, are proportionally segregated from the rest of the city in direct correlation to the average income of their residents. Their most precarious population consists of a working class composed of people whose parents and/ or grandparents were subjected to colonisation in the Maghreb, West Africa or the Caribbean. Here again, structural racism finds in architecture and territorial organisation a particularly effective embodiment. Part of these apparatuses materialises in the relationship of the residents and the national police. A look at the police stations built after the 2005 and 2007 suburban revolts in the Northern and Eastern banlieues is evocative. The particular care put into the materiality and spatiality of these buildings reveals them to be the work of architecture offices, some of which are relatively well known. These buildings, however, hardly hide the antagonism developed by the police towards the

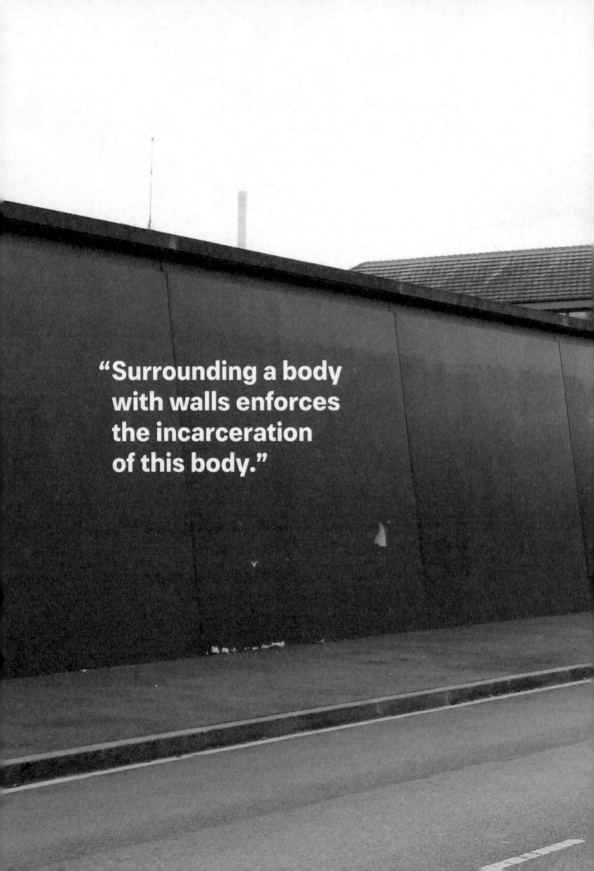

population that surround them: they are small bastions fantasising a future civil war against the racialised youth of France.

Previous page: Police station of Villiers-le-Bel (Northern Paris banlieue), 2015. © Léopold Lambert

This page: Palestinian qasr disobeying the Israeli military's occupation legislation. Project by Léopold Lambert (2010) for *Weaponized Architecture: The Impossibility of Innocence* (dpr-barcelona, 2012)

At a smaller scale, we can see how segregation between bodies is also active through architecture, this time categorising them into two distinct genders to which specific activities have been attributed. A look at the typical post-war American suburban house in relation to the representation of standard gendered bodies, Joe and Josephine, conceived by designer Henry Dreyfuss says a lot about such normative separation. While vehicle compartments and office furniture are calibrated on a male standardised body (Joe), ironing boards, vacuum cleaners and kitchens are calibrated on its female counterpart (Josephine), thus accomplishing what Dreyfuss himself calls "human engineering" in the reinforcement of gender normativity both in terms of anatomy and activity.

Although the ideologies behind the political programmes exposed here were not invented by architecture, architecture is a necessary means to implement their violence on bodies. In this regard, this discipline and its practitioners are complicit and co-responsible for their effects on society. Acknowledging that certain degree of violence is inevitable, as we saw above, a politically conscious architecture will not shy away from it, but rather wonder against what this violence should be oriented. In other words, to what political programme does the architect contribute through construction? We should not be looking to "solve" anything, but rather, to further problematise political situations and engage architectural means of resistance against it. ■

"A politically conscious architecture will not shy away from violence, but rather wonder against what it should be oriented."

Intimate Infra-structures

**A social and spatial
strategy for high-density
design at a human scale**

By Natasha Reid

Intimate Infrastructures

A social and spatial strategy for high-density design at a human scale

By Natasha Reid

"These *intimate* ideas of living emphasise the connections, relationships and interactions between people from the scale of the home to the community."

In search of creative solutions to London's burgeoning housing crisis, Natasha Reid looks at redesigning the classic townhouse typology as mixed-use with communal facilities better suited to the city's diverse needs and changing demographics.

Natasha Reid Design

Natasha Reid founded her studio in 2014 with the aim of enriching the practice of design through a closer focus on how people experience, relate to and perceive their surroundings, with a heightened sensitivity to human nature and behaviour.

The studio has worked with a wide range of clients, from individuals to local authorities, leading developers, cultural institutions and arts organisations including the UN High Commission for Refugees and the British Council. Their *Intimate Infrastructure* project won an international competition in 2015 for solutions to the housing crisis and was presented to the office of the Mayor of London in the context of informing future policy. They were also awarded funding in 2016 for their Intimate Neighbourhoods LDN*NYC initiative – to work in partnership with leading experts and institutions in New York and develop new cross-city insights on placemaking.

In response to the housing crisis in London, Intimate Infrastructures proposes a toolkit and strategy for locking together social, cultural and economic values into a framework for human-centric housing delivery. By addressing the challenges of contemporary living and changing situations, the project proposes new models for accommodating twenty-first century patterns of life. These more "intimate" ideas of living have an emphasis on the connections, relationships and interactions between people, from the scale of the home to that of the community.

Previous page:
Juxtaposing domestic scale with new infrastructure.
© Natasha Reid

This page: Reintepretation of the townhouse.
© Natasha Reid

The project challenges the pervasive model of residential towers. It asks how we can build at high density, using an alternative model, by proposing a strategy for maximising available land use to provide an economic housing solution for different groups in need, yet without incurring the formidable build costs of high-rise.

The proposal is to capitalise on the land available within the city, to allow for urban intensification rather than sprawl, exploring ways of working at large scale, which also pay attention to quality of life, urban vitality, character of place and civic relations.

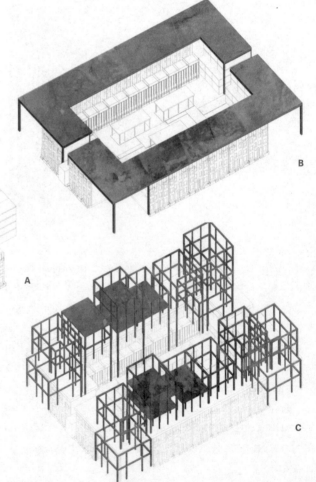

Toolkit for Modular Typologies
and Spatial Principles:
A Shared courtyard
and townhouse terraces
B Elevated shared ground
C Adaptable framework
© Natasha Reid

The project focuses on two groups: local communities
at risk from radical urban renewal and vulnerable to
displacement, and private renters who cannot access home
ownership in the current crisis, from young professionals
on low incomes to other more vulnerable and mobile city
dwellers.

*Mixing old
and new typologies*

A *missing typology* of new-build shared housing is
proposed to meet the demand of renters in the immediate
term, whilst also accommodating larger family homes
within a framework that focuses on quality of place. The
study explores how different types of people can be mixed
in a development rather than creating a mono-tenure
"ghetto".

Currently, the private rental market is unregulated
in terms of space standards. Intimate Infrastructures
proposes new, mass-produced, modular "shared houses"
as standardised components, to ensure minimum space
standard levels, while speeding up delivery and reducing
construction costs.

The *shared house* modules are low-cost, robust shell
spaces, which can be finished by inhabitants according to
their means. This new model could also provide a radical
approach to giving access to property and security by
allowing for micro units of space to be owned too, such as
a single bedroom.

Permanent infrastructure is provided at ground level in
the form of courtyards and owner-occupied townhouses,
based on the London pattern of squares, and aims to
embed the importance of street-life into areas undergoing
change. The townhouse typology is an updated version
of the traditional London terrace, proven to be a highly

London street life

119

resilient and adaptable model in the city fabric. The spatial configuration responds to the changing nature of family structures and work patterns, for instance the increase in adult children returning to the family home in the face of the housing crisis.

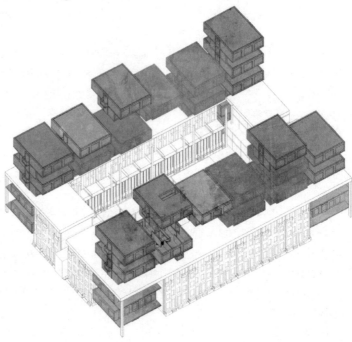

Toolkit for Modular Typologies and Spatial Principles: shared house typologies.
© Natasha Reid

An adaptable frame structure above street level contains the shared homes, which can change, grow and recede according to future needs. Within this, individual dwellings are articulated and vertical elements give rhythm to the street and a human scale to the city – differentiating them from the usual model for mass housing of monolithic, uniform blocks.

Communities of place

The collision of different tenures and groups reflects the heterogeneous city; the proposal provides a range of different conditions to suit people at different stages in life, incomes and lifestyle preferences. It seeks to interlock two types of community, not "pepper potting" them but allowing opportunities for interaction through mixing space for social activities. In order to create a closer, denser layout of households, shared space is emphasised and privacy provided by the careful treatment of boundaries.

This framework approach provides the physical infrastructure for urban densification, while simultaneously setting up a social infrastructure to support strong communities. The project considers the in-between spaces to be as important as the buildings themselves. The areas between interior and exterior allow for overlapping spaces and functions, and subsequently different social groups. Shared spaces are provided for people to appropriate and collectively shape, increasing the number of their chance encounters and facilitating wider participation in civic and communal life.

Building connectedness

"This project considers the in-between spaces to be as important as the buildings themselves."

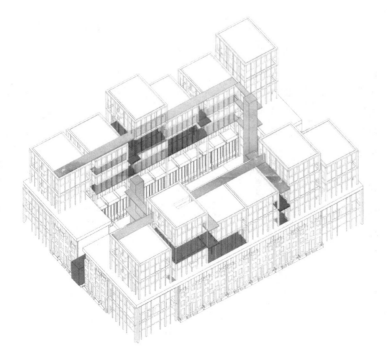

Toolkit for Modular Typologies and Spatial Principles: network of passages and "inbetween" spaces. © Natasha Reid

Typologial relationships

Previous page:
New shared house typology.
© Natasha Reid

The two house typologies have been developed to define much more than a particular appearance or aesthetic. Boundaries are the means to generate both privacy and community in both house types. Using social relations as the generator for design, the built fabric informs how inhabitants meet through creating settings and graded thresholds that delineate the borders between public and private realms. A range of spatial devices across interior and exterior conditions determines the relationships between households and even between members of the same household.

Overall, the project is an exploration of how the arrangement of space can reflect and support relationships from the individual to the civic. Seeking to go deeper than surface appearances and form, it puts forward an architecture that can act as a facilitator of activity and a collective framework for public life. ■

Ruinflatables

Repurposing municipal ruins with residential bubbles

By Andrej Strehovec

Ruinflatables

Repurposing municipal ruins with residential bubbles

By Andrej Strehovec

"It is easy to build a house-object, but the way of life is hard to change ... the challenge for the twenty-first century is infrastructure... architecture is not important." *

*Marjetica Potrč
on Radio Student Ljubljana,
December 2012

In the spirit of the 1970s blow-up experiments by Haus-Rucker-Co, architect Andrej Strehovec's inflatable IN-HABIT-ON capsules are a speculative proposal for bringing life back into municipal ruins.

Andrej Strehovec

Andrej Strehovec is a graduate of the Faculty for Architecture at the University of Ljubljana. He has been a practicing architect since 2003, working on projects which have included public buildings and housing as well as interior design. He founded Strehovec Architecture in 2014. Since 2010, he has been a regular contributor to *Piranesi* magazine (Central-European Architectural Magazine for the Culture of the Environment), writing in the field of architectural theory, while also contributing online and to radio discussions on the subject. He is an active collaborator and exhibitor internationally working on intermedia art projects at the intersection between the humanities and natural science.

IN-HABIT-ON is an experimental concept for future dwelling possibilities that integrates technologically autonomous inflatable capsules into abandoned municipal infrastructure with the ambition of establishing an emancipatory society.

As western society continues with its need to build, arrange and decorate new living environments, IN-HABIT-ON proposes a practice of habitation that is enacted within the rehabilitation of abandoned settlements. Existing, healthy structures are reused and abandoned infrastructure is repaired or hacked.

Instead of producing new building materials, a technologically autonomous, portable, inflatable module is developed: IN-HABIT-ON. It provides a secondary shelter

Previous page: IN-HABIT-ON Cyprus. Graphics: Andrej Strehovec and Sanja Bilinović. Photo: Imgur

This page: IN-HABIT-ON Antwerpen. Graphics: Andrej Strehovec and Sanja Bilinović. Photo: Dan Marbaix

shell, enabling integration within old built-structures, which act as primary construction shells. This new infrastructural architecture incorporates neo-eclecticism, technology driven design and hacked communal infrastructure.

"The future will be utopian, or there will be none." *

*Slavoj Žižek,
The Reality of the Virtual,
2004

The capsule-like shells of IN-HABIT-ON are made of a multi-layered synthetic material that provides structural stability. This inflated hard-wall material is already in use in the boat industry. Inner and outer layers of the hard-wall are made from cut-resistant and air-tight polyvinyl chloride (PVC) fabric. These two layers are connected by a strong PVC yarn, forming a sandwich-like membrane. When this membrane is inflated with air under very high pressure, it provides an extremely solid surface that can withstand puncture and impact. It also functions as an insulation wall, maintaining and preserving the microclimate of the interior.

PVC membrane is fully recyclable and ideal for reprocessing. It is also inexpensive to make, requires minimal maintenance when in use, and is extremely durable. It is commonly used to make long-lasting products, often with a life expectancy exceeding 60 years. Thanks to its unique polymer structure, it is well suited for mechanical and feedstock recycling when it comes to the end of its life. Feedstock recycling is where waste is broken right back down into its basic chemical molecules, which can then be used again to make PVC or other plastics. This enables the production of a new module by simply using the remains of the old one if necessary.

Each IN-HABIT-ON module is an inflatable membrane, with auto-open-vacuum-gap, it has a condensation and bio-filter device to collect water, a sewage filtration device, an energy bacteria laboratory in combination with solar-energy generator and an ultra-sonic personal shower.

The IN-HABIT-ON would be lightweight and easy to transport by a personal electric vehicle.

IN-HABIT-ON reinstates habitation as a priority over the museological or historicist approach of preserving architecture solely for cultural or luxury purposes. The project addresses pre-existing structures, abandoned for varying reasons, and reveals possibilities for their sustainable rehabilitation and upgrade with minimal environmental impact using minimum energy or logistical input. It combines temporary lifestyles – such as squatting or camping – with progressive technology and life values.

As shown in the accompanying images, the chosen sites have some common characteristics: they present abandoned building locations, both within settlements or a public spaces. The structure of the abandoned buildings needs to be stable, or at least offer a fair possibility of remediation. The chosen sites should also provide some kind of desirable public or natural environment that offers potential for easy restoration and implementation. Existing municipal water supplies, sewage systems, electricity cables and urban context are also part of the necessary basis for rehabilitation of old settlements.

The site in Novi Sad, Serbia, for example, presents a tower block – formerly a workers' university – which was left derelict after a fire in 2000 and has been abandoned ever since despite its central location in the city. Utilising the skyscraper's construction and internal infrastructure, the IN-HABIT-ON capsules could be used as temporary shelters in this concentrated urban area. The shelters can help to prevent social degradation and stagnation within the city centre as well as maintain other local public services until the full restoration of the building.

The same temporary inhabitation and maintenance concept could be applied to the site in Antwerp, Belgium. This case study is located in the interior of the nineteenth-century neo-gothic Stock Exchange building. The first stock exchange building in the world, originally built in 1531, it was destroyed by fire and reconstructed in 1872 but has been closed since 2003 due to modern fire regulations.

The site in Varosha, Cyprus, was a modern tourist area that had been left uninhabited since the Turkish invasion in 1974, and the fishing village site at Shengshan (China) was abandoned because of the diversification of economic production, which had a catastrophic impact on the local fishing industry. Both sites are located in a warm climate, which is attractive for tourism. IN-HABIT-ON capsules could be used to establish new tourist infrastructure, or provide a living environment for a community.

IN-HABIT-ON provides a platform for projecting future human existence, establishing values of a technologically and culturally developed society. The platform offers a solution through criticism of the existing consumerist social establishment, redundancy of social development

Previous page: IN-HABIT-ON
Infrastructure. Graphics:
Andrej Strehovec. Photo: Hei
Jiaoshi, Imaginechina, Corbis

This page: IN-HABIT-ON
Neoplanta. Image: Andrej
Strehovec

politics, criticism of corporate driven migrations, with
an idea of the establishment of a future autonomous,
emancipatory society. The project also stimulates the
establishment of temporary but high quality environments
for living, which can respond to the needs of the nomadic
societies arising from ever-increasing global migration. ■

Being Guerilla Architects

Hacking the city and reclaiming social spaces

By Guerilla Architects

Being Guerilla Architects

Hacking the city and reclaiming social spaces

By Guerilla Architects

"Form is not a given architectural parameter of style anymore, but a consequence of our actions."

With their transgressive yet playful approach, the Guerilla Architects collective seeks to facilitate new interactions in public space with creative interventions: from window cleaning to a co-working space in a caravan.

Guerilla Architects' philosophy is to seek out and uncover the potential that is hidden and ignored within our society and built environments. We are looking for the in-between spaces and the grey areas: legal, political, social or spatial. We founded our collective in London and Berlin in 2012 in order to work autonomously and subversively without restrictive requirements. To be able to preserve the architectural quality of our projects, to choose the right spaces and declare their potential, we must utilise new methods of working. As an international collective working on the forgotten and unused resources of our cities, we remain diverse in our daily work and widely spread in our cultural habitats. Guerilla Architects combine the professional backgrounds of architecture, urban planning, research, art history, art production, interior design, scenography and theatre, located across Germany, Bulgaria and Italy.

Our working method is fundamentally a process of brainstorming once a week in regular Skype meetings between our various home cities across Europe. This is a condensed form of exchange enabling the allocation of tasks, on the basis of everyone's preferences, for project-related fieldwork. Therefore a project is always a process of collective decisions. That's why we also consider involving impulses from "outside", especially from local residents at a particular site or potential end-users of an intervention.

Guerilla Architects

Guerilla Architects are an international collective of architects focusing on the forgotten and unused resources of our cities. Sharing a common squatting experience in London in 2012, the name "Guerilla Architects" evolved through the need to defend ourselves in court. We are a loose collective of thinkers, makers, theorists, planners, pedants and muddlers, who range in-between the fields of urban planning, built and temporary architectures, art production, cultural history, theatre and art. We come from different parts of Germany, Italy and Bulgaria and are based in Berlin, Göttingen, Sofia, as well as soon in London.

"A project is always a process of collective decisions."

We think of our projects not just as outcomes of our designs, but as frameworks for a process in which we can find a better result in the end. The "end" should not be determined by a deadline, but in how far we can imagine and foster change through our intervention.

We therefore envisage and plan a project backwards from the supposed "end" to the beginning. What do we want to have achieved when we are finished? What did we change? What kind of images (as formal and aesthetic documentation of our work, but also in the minds of citizens/ residents/ end-users) do we want to have produced?

Architecture should not be determined by abstract concepts; it should be determined by precisely the thing that it is designed for. Form is not a given architectural parameter of style anymore, but a consequence of our actions.

"Public space" is supposed to be "social space" in cities, for its citizens. But it is also related to the space of the state or government that owns it. The participation of the public of course plays a key role in activating public spaces, however, it also can help ordinary people to realise their power to mould their environments around their own needs, whether their neighbourhood, city or country.

To investigate the possibilities of a social space within its legal and political framework, it is necessary not just to think about public plazas or transportation systems, which should be open to all. Unused wastelands, vacant structures, modern ruins or even rivers and lakes have the potential to be transformed into something fundamentally public. Further, now that the virtual world has become a real public space for interaction and exchange and where the foundation of free action is information, the general idea of public space should not just be limited by spatial borders, but should also be considered as a state of mind that reaches into the political sphere and holds within it the possibility to act freely.

Pages 136-37 and this page: Hidden Borough performance cleaning windows. © Guerilla Architects

Hidden Borough, one of our projects at a squat in Great Suffolk Street, London, gave a Victorian warehouse back to the city and its citizens by simply cleaning its windows. Our temporary home became open to the public and symbolised our goal: that urban space belongs to everyone and can be redefined. Disconnecting the city from the logic of money, standardisation and regulation, we then staged a utopia of freely available resources such as shelter, water, food, electricity. Whilst small urban interventions alone have a nominal and very local impact, amidst a much wider network of interventions interconnected to form a new borough, they could help provide a model for a new method of urban planning policy. This new urban district, made up of vacancies, has no fixed borders. It acts like a synaptic net: it is not closed, but open to all and expandable.

Hidden Borough net.
© Guerilla Architects

Since that common experience, we have worked on several
issues around the topic of unused and forgotten resources.
In particular the specific issue of food overproduction.
The Diver – Restaurant Experience, for example, was a social
experiment to provide strangers with an unusual dinner
experience. Creating a fancy pop-up restaurant in various
vacant sites, such as an ex-Soviet broadcasting centre
in Berlin, we aimed to interfere with typical culinary
expectations. When our guests got their bills, they
realised our true intentions as all our unconventional,
vegetarian, four-course menu was made and cooked from
waste food.

On another occasion, a market square served as a starting
point for an impromptu intervention called *Gefundenes
Fressen (Donation Dinner)*. Shortly before the end of the
market, we asked the market traders to donate their
leftovers for a common dinner. We cooked several
meals and everybody was invited to join the dining
table. Thereby a simple meal of leftover food became
a sculptural installation of social interaction. We used

the existing structures and network of this particular public space and gave its users, who came from various backgrounds, a new platform for communication without barriers. The empty table remained at the end as the only evidence of what had temporarily emphasised the market square's key function – as a place of social exchange.

Gefundes Fressen: empty table remains as evidence of the event. © Guerilla Architects

Our most recent project, *Bastian, der StadtSymbiont (Bastian in the City)* – a co-working space inside a caravan – is another attempt to hack the city. With rising rent prices for studio spaces, the creative industries face increasingly unstable working conditions. Despite this, or maybe just because of it, many creatives are striving harder still to achieve the dream of having an autonomous space for their own practice. By working "between the gaps" in laws and parking regulations, we developed a guide for central, long-lasting and cost-efficient working spaces. Free wifi, public toilets and canteens complete this autonomous, always on-site, long-term and cheap architecture office as well as connecting this small-scale working space to the scale of the city at large. Always in movement, the architect's workspace and field of work merge on site.

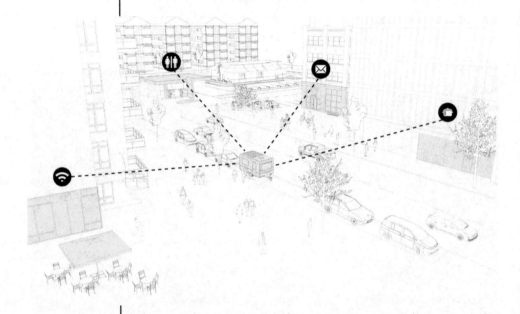

Bastian in the City: a mobile co-working space in a caravan. © Guerilla Architects

The future of architecture does not lie in our hands, but it can be actively developed by working collectively, by being politically engaged and by being internationally connected.

See you on the road! ■

Adapting Tradition for the Future

Fostering sustainability and a local sense of ownership

By Jan Glasmeier

Adapting Tradition for the Future
Fostering sustainability and a local sense of ownership

By Jan Glasmeier

"One of our main aims is to involve members of migrant communities living close by in the construction process, thereby fostering a local sense of ownership."

Jan Glasmeier of a.gor.a architects describes how the educational projects they help build, working with marginalised groups, community-based organisations and NGOs along the Thai-Burma border and in Chiang Mai, take advantage of established patterns of building whilst incorporating innovations that come from their own training and background in Europe.

Jan Glasmeier

Jan Glasmeier moved to Thailand in 2012 where he founded a.gor.a architects with Albert Company Olmo. He is currently working at Mae Tao clinic and volunteering for several community-based organisations. He was a lead architect for Arup Singapore during the construction of the Singapore Sports Hub and worked for Foster + Partners in London on the Masdar City masterplan in Abu Dhabi, UAE. Glasmeier graduated in 2006 with a Diploma (Dipl. Ing.) in Architecture from the Technical University of Darmstadt in Germany.

Previous page: Temporary dormitory - interior view.
© a.gor.a architects

This page: Temporary dormitory - front view.
© a.gor.a architects

Training Centre for Mae Tao Clinic

With an armed conflict having persisted for decades in the Karen State of Myanmar – between the Burmese government and the minority Karen ethnic group who want more autonomy – a daily flow of refugees and immigrants to neighbouring Thailand has resulted. In the Thai town of Mae Sot, a few kilometres from the Burmese border, numerous schools and orphanages offer accommodation and education for the refugees and immigrants. One of these, under the tutelage of the Mae Tao Clinic organisation, which provides free healthcare for Burmese refugees and migrants, is the Children's Development Centre school (CDC) which hosts more than 800 students.

The clinic commissioned us to design and construct a new training centre for the school. This is planned as a campus of several buildings – including a classroom and temporary dormitories – that will be grouped together on a piece of land not far from the old Mae Tao Clinic site.

The lack of space, and in many cases, the need for immediate accommodation for new students, meant that the school required a new model for a temporary low-cost dormitory that would be easy to assemble and could be built using recycled materials wherever possible.

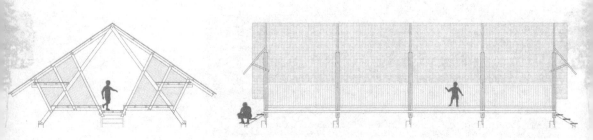

Temporary dormitory:
elevation and section.
© a.gor.a architects

The dormitory structure that we designed has a capacity for 25 residents, its interior layout providing an open and airy space, while still offering semi-privacy and storage space for the every student. The building materials used are locally available and familiar to their users, thus allowing for easy maintenance and low maintenance costs and also mean that the building fits well into its local environment. Funded by the Embassy of Luxembourg in Bangkok, the first of four planned dormitories was built in April 2012 within a space of four weeks.

The main cost of the building is the structure, made from recycled timber, which represents 70 per cent of the total construction cost – and which can be re-sold in the future for 80 per cent of the price. Bamboo and thatch are used for walls, floors, and roofs. Although these materials are not designed to last for more than two years without any pre-treatment, they are easily available every season – and thus the cost is an affordable and relatively stable one for the local community.

The recycled timber used for the dormitories comes from old buildings in town, from which it is carefully stripped out and put to one side by the demolition crews. The timber is polished, de-nailed and sawn down to the correct size. The frame structure is designed to be easy to disassemble and reassemble later at a new location.

The quality of available timber, mainly teak, along the Thai-Burma border is said to be amongst the best in the world. However, the price of timber has risen by over 300 per cent over the last few years due to deforestation and illegal trafficking along the border. Thus recycling timber has become popular among the local people in order to reduce the cost of a new building. Using timber as a main building material enables us as architects to help preserve the traditional construction skills of local people already familiar with the material.

Funded by APHEDA – Union Aid Abroad from Australia – the construction of the two classrooms and a library building of 200 square metres started in September 2011 and was completed by July 2012. For this project we co-operated very closely with Gyaw Gyaw, an organisation founded by Norwegian landscape architect Line Ramstad, which works to build social buildings for and with the minority Karen ethnic group.

"The building materials used are locally available and familiar to their users, thus allowing for easy maintenance and low maintenance costs."

The buildings were placed to minimise any negative environmental impact and reduce their energy consumption. The orientation of the buildings and the location of windows within them follows the main wind direction, allowing air to flow through the houses and cool down the inside of the buildings, without the additional use of air-conditioning or fans.

For the construction of the buildings, adobe bricks and second hand timber was chosen to ensure that the majority of the materials employed were either reused, recycled or could in time be returned to the ground without any further damage to the environment.

Training centre: front view.
© a.gor.a architects

Adobe, as a natural and environmentally friendly material, was used for both the classroom and office walls. To protect these walls from the impact of standing water, a 30 cm raised concrete slab, had to be built first as a base. The roof is of timber construction with composite roof tiles. The windows and doors, also made out of recycled timber, were later painted green and blue for the classroom and ochre for the office building. Again

Training centre: rear view.
© a.gor.a architects

the materials used were all available locally and well known to their users, allowing for ease of maintenance and resulting in low costs. Adobe bricks have been used in Thailand for many years. The value of using them to construct walls is not only based on environmental and economic reasons: mud is also an easy material to work with and allows everybody in the community to participate in the construction process. Due to its composition and thickness, earthen walls are durable yet biodegradable. They provide sufficient thermal mass to the buildings to ensure excellent thermal performance and other beneficial attributes such as sound and fireproofing.

In late 2012, we were contacted by the headmaster of the Karen Migrant Learning Centre in Mae Sot. This schooling project is supporting and educating around 450 migrant children from the Karen community of Mae Sot. The school had to move from its then current site as the landowner decided not to extend its lease after May 2014. To ensure that the school would be able to continue its education programme, a new site had to be found and a new school built within two years.

Kwel Ka Baung Migrant Learning Centre

Casira, an organisation from Quebec, Canada, was able to raise funds for this project over a two-year period. Casira also travelled to Thailand in 2012 and 2013, participating in two workshops, each lasting four weeks. In June 2014, the Kwel Kah Baung School's new campus opened and the students moved into their new classrooms.

Previous page: Kwel Ka Baung: inside the classroom © a.gor.a architects

This page: Kwel Ka Baung: central corridor © a.gor.a architects

One of our main aims in all the projects is to involve members of migrant communities living close by in the construction process, thereby fostering a local sense of ownership of the project and ensuring that future maintenance can be done without external support. For the building material, adobe was chosen for this project, which perfectly matches the challenges of a tropical climate: ensuring the interior is kept cool through the day and requiring minimum maintenance after the rainy season.

a.gor.a architects aims is to learn from traditional Thai architecture, so that it can offer an attractive alternative to more common (un)architectural solutions. Given the steady pace of development and the increasing spread and use of cheap industrialised materials and techniques – such as concrete, often ill-advisedly deployed – what a.gor.a pursues is a vernacular hybrid. The architects take advantage of established patterns of building and tried-and-tested construction techniques, then enriches them with ideas and innovations coming from their training and background in Europe, which are then developed and tested on site. Such a blend tends to be a more climate-responsive, ecological and economical one than the architecture that too often nowadays is fueling urban development in Thailand. a.gor.a's mission is to widen the range of possible solutions and to communicate this potential to the community they work with/in. This approach implies the use of strictly local materials and the training of selected workers to be actively involved in the design process.

Although there has been a recent increase in architects working in areas affected by natural disaster and war, our approach is very different. We are not architects working in an emergency situation. Some of the migrant communities in Thailand have existed for decades and we believe that it's important to have a sensitive, considered approach to local and cultural conditions and variations. It is not about helping people in need. It is about sharing experience and learning from each other. And through this confluence of local and "western" knowledge, as well as through the use of local materials, you can create a completely new form of architecture as can be seen in the work that we are doing. ▪

"What a.gor.a pursues is a vernacular hybrid."

Telling Tales

Storytelling
as architectural
representation

By Jana Čulek

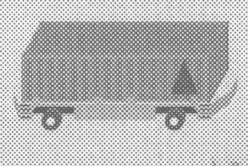

Telling Tales

Storytelling as architectural representation

By Jana Čulek

"As architects, we often create more stories than buildings. "

With her research project "A Flat Tale", architect and urbanist Jana Čulek analyses the phenomenon of storytelling in representing Dutch architecture in a series of three books, analysing and exploring how both visual and textual narrative can explain architecture.

As architects, we often create more stories than buildings. We have come to a point where the main criterion for a scheme's success is a compelling concept, manifested through the architectural story. *A Flat Tale* is a research project that examines architectural stories, their narrative structures and methods, through the specific investigation of Dutch architecture and visual culture.

Jana Čulek

Jana Čulek is an architect and urbanist living and working in the Netherlands. Originally from Zagreb, Croatia, she graduated from the Zagreb Faculty of Architecture in 2013. In early 2016 she completed the postgraduate master's programme at the Berlage Center for Advanced Studies in Architecture and Urban Design in Delft, Netherlands. Her thesis project, *A Flat Tale*, has been exhibited and published as a part of the Berlage Generation XXV graduation event titled "Scenes from the Good Life". Parts of the project are also a published in the *Fairy Tales: Volume 3* book, produced for the similarly named competition organised by Blank Space. Her most recent design and research projects have been focusing on the topic of architectural representation and narrative methods.

Previous page: A Flat Tale: "Exporting Architecture" © Jana Čulek

This page: A Flat Tale Book Set. Clockwise from top left: Pitch, A Reference Unreferenced, A Flat Tale and A Good Life ABC. Photo: Lena Giovanazzi

The project questions the storytelling capacity of architecture by using a research and projective method in which a known category of architectural representation is paired with a familiar literary and didactic genre. The format of the story is used as an heuristic device to extrapolate and transpose different approaches to narrative structures and methods onto architectural narratives. This method has resulted in three component publications: an alphabet book entitled *A Good Life ABC*; an architectural picture book called *A Flat Tale*; and an architectural journal appropriately titled *Pitch*. The three parts represent three phases in the development of narratives and architectural projects, as well as three different ways of correlating text and image. The project concludes with an appendix, *A Reference Unreferenced*, which explains the correlations and thoughts behind the project's texts and drawings.

A Good Life ABC:
"G is for Glasshouse".
Photo: Lena Giovanazzi

A Good Life ABC is an architectural alphabet book. Designed to be analogous to the way architecture is presented to the public, it represents the simplest way to give and receive knowledge. Intending to make projects

A Good Life ABC:
"L is for Landscape".
Photo: Lena Giovanazzi

easier to understand, architects sometimes oversimplify. In an effort to explain the complex architectural idea in a relatable way, the architectural process is reduced to a set of simplified drawings and an icon that represents the final stage of development. *A Good Life* ABC uses letters of the alphabet, paired with drawings of familiar objects and elements of the Dutch built environment, drawn in a reductive manner with minimal detailing. In order to further remove any specificity from the objects, the colour palette is reduced to primary shades. In this way emblematic objects and places are created which refer only to themselves and perform as generic symbols of Dutch identity.

As an analogy to the architectural project, the second book, *A Flat Tale*, is presented in the form of a picture book. "Picture books are unified artistic wholes in which text and pictures, covers and end pages, and the details of design, work together to provide an aesthetically satisfying experience. The spelling *picturebook* – as one word – is utilised intentionally in order to emphasise the unity of words and pictures that is the most important

"Unlike the picture book, where both the drawing and the text are used as critical and didactic tools, the architectural drawing has become mere representation."

1 Sipe, Lawrence R. "Picture-books as Aesthetic Objects". *Literacy Teaching and Learning*, Volume 6, Number 1. pp.23-42

2 Nodelman, Perry. *Words About Pictures: The Narrative Art of Children's Picture Books.* University of Georgia Press: 1990

hallmark of this type of book."[1] Picture books use images to illustrate the events of the corresponding *fabula*. Image is used as a conveyor of spatial narrative, while text is used to convey the temporal one. Since "words and pictures necessarily have a combative relationship, their complementarity is a matter of opposites complementing each other by virtue of their differences. As a result, the relationships between pictures and texts in picture books tend to be ironic: each speaks about matters on which the other is silent."[2] But unlike the picture book, where both the drawing and the text are used as critical and didactic tools, the architectural drawing has become mere representation. In order to regain its critical use, the drawing has to perform as something more than just a visual description of a project at hand. It has to become a speculative tool, containing an additional layer of thought and information. In this way, the nature of the architectural drawing can change. In a world that has already been oversaturated with images, the drawing can cease to be a representational end-product and become, once again, part of the process of creating and disseminating architectural thought.

The story depicted in *A Flat Tale* is centred around the development of Almere, the newest city on the youngest Dutch polder. From large areas of housing developments, to the masterplan for Almere Centrum created by the Office for Metropolitan Architecture in 1997, and public buildings designed by other famous Dutch architectural offices, Almere has it all. The story of Almere can be viewed as a compact version of Dutch architectural history, a fruitful resource for creating imagery relating to various aspects of Dutch architectural production. In *A Flat Tale*, Almere is used as a lens for presenting and observing architectural, urban and infrastructural

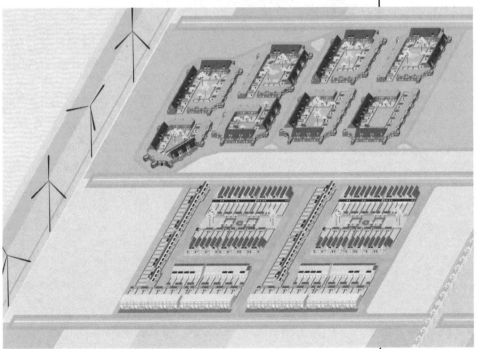

approaches. It is also used to establish ideas forming generative theoretical elements of Dutch architecture and culture (such as concept, export, good life, welfare, subsidies, etc).

Top: A Flat Tale: "Planning Polders". Photo: Lena Giovanazzi

Bottom: A Flat Tale: "Polder Life". © Jana Čulek

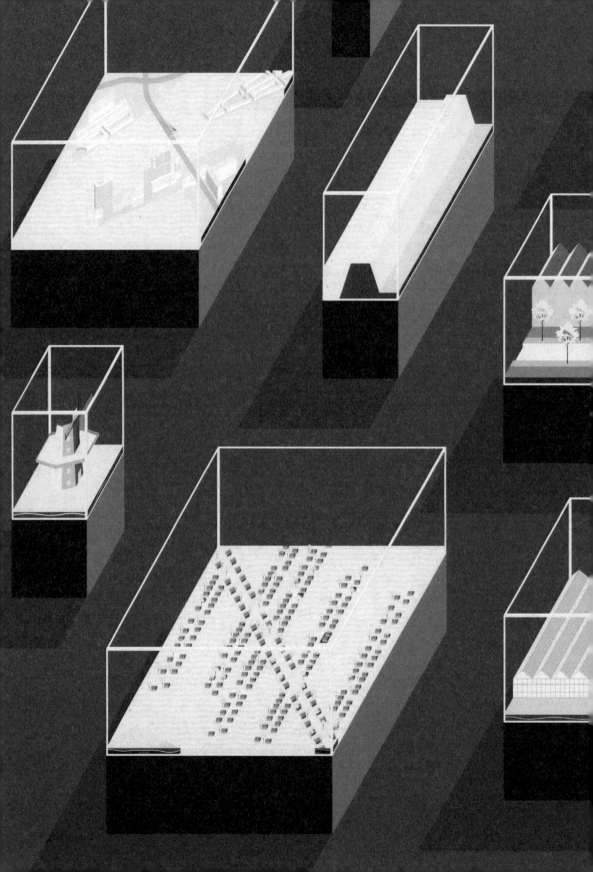

Previous page: A Flat Tale:
"Constructed Landscapes".
© Jana Čulek

Focusing predominantly on architectural texts, the third element, *Pitch*, takes the format of an architectural journal. Composed from texts, paired with simple black and white diagrammatic drawings, it examines Dutch architectural projects through the use of narrative, argumentation and criticism. The format of the architectural journal is almost without exception aimed at architects. When writing about architecture, or related subjects, architects tend to use jargon filled with overly complicated semantic constructs, alluding to a complex, deep and intellectual creative process. But Dutch stories are different. When writing about their projects, Dutch architects tend to use terms, images, words and experiences relatable to everyone. These are stories aimed for the end user and the architectural theoretician or critic. In *Pitch*, these stories are collected and used as case studies in order to re-examine the concepts, diagrams and original project pitches created for some of the most iconic examples of Dutch architecture.

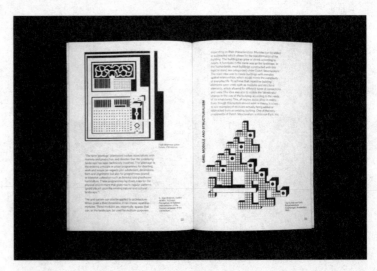

Pitch: "Grid, Module
and Structuralism".
Photo: Lena Giovanazzi

Pitch ends with a fictional conclusion, an interpretation of the same type of material, but through a written description of an architectural project.[3] It is set in an undefined future. It is a utopian, infrastructural, urban and architectural project for a mountain in the Netherlands. The description excludes all the visual elements that typically define architectural projects in order to question if it can still remain accessible, relatable and understandable even without the use of graphic tools of representation. It questions the capacity of architectural storytelling by presenting an architectural project, which is inherently visual, only through text. Diagrams and allusions to the project in the form of 'infiltrators' are placed in the first two publications in order to entice the reader to re-examine the entire set after finishing the first read.

3 "The Appendix should be regarded as a fictional conclusion, an interpretation of the same material, but not through words, but in a series of architectural projects." Koolhaas, Rem. *Delirious New York*. New York: The Monacelli Press, 1994

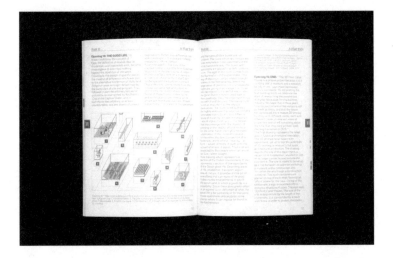

A Reference Unreferenced: "Part 2: A Flat Tale". Photo: Lena Giovanazzi

A Reference Unreferenced is the project's appendix. It contains references, sources, inspirations and explanations for all three elements of the project. The appendix draws on the research carried out on Dutch architecture and visual culture: the history, meaning and structure of tales and narratives and the approaches, elements, meanings, structures and formats of picture books. Formatted as a reference lexicon, it illuminates the stories and backgrounds behind the texts and drawings, positioning them in the architectural discourse and giving them an added meaning, which can be explored through re-examining the entire set.

By merging existing visual and lexical narrative forms with methods of architectural representation, a different set of rules is applied to forming and sharing architectural thought. Examining architectural representation through both its lexical and visual qualities allowed for the elucidation of three main categories forming this project: the diagram and emblematic object presented through the alphabet book; the architectural design project and its narrative presented through the picture book; and the architectural journal with its short story conclusion. These elements, together with the appendix, represent the symbols, depiction, reflection and story of the good life in the Netherlands. ■

Walk
& Hórreo

Remote farm buildings
as new economic drivers

By Ignacio Gias

Walk & Hórreo

Remote farm buildings as new economic drivers

By Ignacio Gias

"A stable economy needs constantly to rethink itself, applying strong doses of self-criticism."

A project aiming to show how disused buildings remaining from outdated farming practices – here the grain stores of Northern Spain – could form the basis for a new network of cultural tourism.

Ignacio Gias

Ignacio Gias was born in Madrid in 1985 and graduated in architecture at the CEU San Pablo University, Madrid in 2010. He founded his own architecture practice, Nacho Gias Studio, in 2014, which works at the intersection of architecture, communication and new technology.

It's no secret that the turnover and economic dimensions of the art market are a strong index of the prosperity of a society. One could say that the more developed a society is and the more prosperous an economy it has, then the greater its art market too. France is a clear example of this. Let's raise two theories as to why the most stable economies have stronger cultural industries: one theory is that when people have an economic surplus and are in a position to save money, they can afford to become art consumers. This encourages the development of a class of cultural producers – artists – whose work then has a stable and accessible market niche. Another theory, towards which I lean, sees culture and creativity as a fountain providing water and sustenance to all the other sectors of the economy and making them prosper. A stable economy needs constantly to rethink itself, applying strong doses of self-criticism. It needs the space for reflection, creativity and criticism offered by culture.

Europe is aiming to become an engine of ideas, a space of creativity where the value of mechanical production processes is decreasing while the workload of the knowledge economy increases. The European middle classes are increasingly able to reinvent themselves according to market trends. I myself believe that the creative economy is the only path to freedom and personal development for us as citizens, a tool that provides us with the flexibility needed to help us face the great changes in society and economy, such as globalisation, financial crisis and migration.

Previous page: Repaired and glazed *hórreo.* © Nacho Gias Studio

Above: Hórreo in Valongo,
Galicia, Spain.
CC BY 2.0 Gabriel González

Below: Hórreo in Quinta
da Bouça, Viseu, Portugal.
© Tiago Ferreirinho

Since the creative economy can constantly reinvent itself, it can adapt to and carry on through each new situation. An illustration of this is my project, *Walk & Hórreo*, which I've been developing in response to the exodus of young people from the countryside to big cities, in Spain and the consequences of this trend on rural areas and heritage. Guided by my convictions, I wanted to look at how creative economic ideas could be used to provide new tools for growth in such wasted, underpopulated rural areas. I've been developing a pilot for the project with the Factoría Cultural in Matadero, Madrid.

Located in the farming regions of Northern Spain, *hórreos* are small wooden structures designed for food preservation that are raised off the ground on stone pillars to prevent animals from accessing them. The first *hórreos* appeared in medieval times and the oldest one still preserved today dates from 1768. Changes in agricultural production and the rural exodus of the local population over the last century have rendered this typology of building useless and as a result most have been destroyed. As *hórreos* are often located in fairly extreme environments they are exposed to hard climatic conditions. The impact of the weather breaks down their structural elements until they collapse. In regions like Cantabria, Northern Spain, or in Sweden and Portugal, they have almost completely disappeared. Those remaining (almost 40,000) are mostly found in Asturias and Galicia, where it is estimated that every day two or three more are disappearing.

Northern Spain has traditionally been an agricultural territory where families used to take care of their own fields. The *hórreo* was the answer to a very specific requirement – that of needing to keep corn cobs and

other crops dry and safe from rodents before they were threshed. During the twentieth century, agricultural production went through a total revolution. Massive companies now own huge fields designed for the industrial production of food. The preservation of the

Sequence of opening timber shutters on a renovated *hórreo*. Render © Nacho Gias Studio

Repaired and glazed *hórreo*.
Render © Nacho Gias Studio

harvest is no longer done in *hórreos* with these large companies using vast storage buildings instead. Hence the abandonment of the *hórreos* to the rain, freezing winter temperatures and strong winds that reduce these heritage structures to heaps of rubble in the mountains.

This project aims to create an infrastructure to help make *hórreo* preservation profitable. The tapping of the consistent existing flows of tourists to the famous pilgrim walking route, the Camino de Santiago de Compostela, is a key element in this strategy. Through the creation of an app, backpackers would be able to locate *hórreos* and spend the night in one of them for a token price. This would contribute to a further objective of this initiative, beyond just heritage preservation, that of giving the opportunity to small farmers to reinvent their profession and economic base by using new technology to take advantage of their unique locations. In a society where young people are leaving the countryside to improve their lives in big cities, and where working practices and social structures in rural communities have remained fixed in the past, Northern

Spain needs new ideas to reinvent itself. This project, beyond its immediate aim, is intended to become a model for economic reactivation and the preservation of both the cultural and natural environment. But this *Walk & Hórreo* proposal, beyond just being a useful strategy linking economic, cultural and environmental aims, is also intended to touch on a sense of mystery, magic and wonder inherent in some of these extraordinary structures.

This project is a step towards an image of what a European future could be like, a future in which both nature and culture play a key role in becoming prosperity creators. ■

Repaired and glazed *hórreo* interior. Render © Nacho Gias Studio

The Bigger Picture

Socially-informed urban transformation

By Aleksandra Zarek

The Bigger Picture

Socially-informed urban transformation

By Aleksandra Zarek

"Cohesive regeneration cannot always be delivered through isolated restorations of single buildings without a larger integrated strategy."

Architect Aleksandra Zarek presents her thesis work: an holistic approach to urban transformation as a basis for socially-informed evolution of cities, increased quality of life and sustainable urban revival focussed on the example of the Kortepohja Student Village in Jyväskylä, Finland.

The problem of adapting and updating old building stock to contemporary living standards is currently being faced by many cities across Europe and beyond. This necessity holds the potential to enhance social sustainability in urban areas. However, cohesive regeneration cannot always be delivered through isolated restorations of single buildings without a larger integrated strategy.

This project involves the transformation of the Student Village in the Kortepohja district of the Finnish city of Jyväskylä, which is the subject of a proposal to renovate and rejuvenate it. The scheme was commissioned by the University of Jyväskylä's Student Union (JYY) and is presently awaiting implementation.

The main goal of the project is to revitalise the existing building stock through a holistic approach at multiple scales, in order to create a high-quality-living environment for students and JYY's staff as well as re-establish the Student Village's presence in the context of Kortepohja and Jyväskylä. The modernist façades of the Village's historic core, designed by Erkki Kantonen's office, were listed and given heritage status in 2008, meaning a sensitive strategy of respectful transformation is required for any renovation.

The project is based on three interlocking scales, which form the framework for a comprehensive, socially-focused

Aleksandra Zarek

Aleksandra Zarek is an architect currently working at award-winning Stephenson Studio in Manchester. Her internationally-oriented experience includes various practices in Berlin, Lisbon and Poland. She was trained at the University of Sheffield and Tampere University of Technology, where she developed an interest in using architectural and urban design as a tool for social engagement and urban transformation.

Her housing vision for the future was awarded a purchase prize by the City of Lahti in the ARA Home 2049 international student design competition.

Previous page: Kortepohja exterior proposal.
© Aleksandra Zarek

revival: a development plan for Kortepohja; a masterplan for the Student Village and a detailed retrofit of the central Rentukka Student Union building.

A university city with the legacy of Alvar Aalto

The city of Jyväskylä is located in central Finland and in the western part of Finnish Lakeland. Jyväskylä University, students from which form the body of the Student Village's residents and a significant proportion

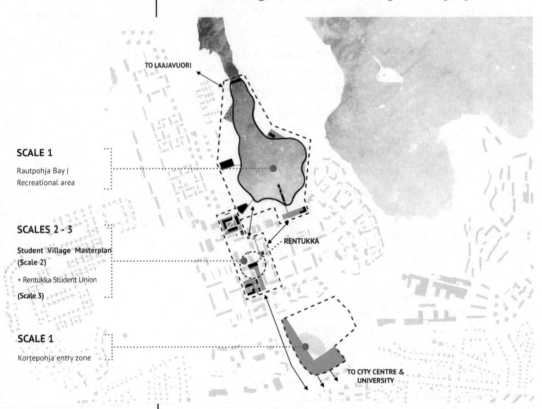

TO LAAJAVUORI

SCALE 1
Rautpohja Bay |
Recreational area

SCALES 2 - 3
Student Village Masterplan
(Scale 2)
+ Rentukka Student Union
(Scale 3)

RENTUKKA

SCALE 1
Kortepohja entry zone

TO CITY CENTRE &
UNIVERSITY

Kortepohja Student Village
plan. © Aleksandra Zarek

of the local population, has been a catalyst for the development of the city and in establishing its national and international reputation.

The university's campus, as well as many other buildings across Jyväskylä, were designed by Alvar Aalto, whose reputation contributes to the international image of the institution and the city. This academic- and design-oriented context provides a strong rationale for the rejuvenation of the village whilst at the same time being designed to enrich students' experience and improving the quality of the built environment.

The first scale of intervention concentrates on the overall development plan for Kortepohja. The district is situated in the north-western part of the city, around three kilometres from its central core and the academic campus.

Scale 1:
Kortepohja District
development plan

Kortepohja aerial view.
© Aleksandra Zarek

The purpose of the scheme at this level is the physical and metaphorical consolidation of new and existing zones within its neighbourhood as well as reconnecting it back into the context of the city.

Kortepohja, whose construction was initiated in the 1960s as a result of the city's and university's growth, constitutes a peaceful residential area. Although it features a number of compelling modernist buildings and recreational zones, the perception of connectivity in the neighbourhood is severely disrupted by many undeveloped sites.

A series of holistic interventions in the district seek to improve the connectivity of its different areas such as the Student Village, the Laajavuori recreational park, the Rautpohja Bay area around the reservoir, or the entry zone to Kortepohja from the city centre. The scheme provides a detailed recreational proposal around the Rautpohja reservoir while suggesting the future development of the entry zone as an area of extended student housing.

The interventions around Rautpohja refresh its image as a scenic reservoir with significant wildlife. A boardwalk links the network of facilities, such as an observation pier, a public sauna, educational centre with allotments and open-air theatre, stimulating a rich and diverse recreational experience. This both enhances opportunities to contemplate the natural environment whilst offering leisure opportunities for students and local residents. The route could be extended to other adjacent areas, such as Laajavuori or around the Haukanniemi peninsula, emphasising the district's integrated character.

Scale 2:
Kortepohja Student
Village masterplan

The Kortepohja Student Village, located in the heart of Kortepohja, forms the subject of the second scale of development. The village constitutes multiple layers of development embedded in the context of the city's and university's growth. Its modernist core, with five high-rise blocks and the central Rentukka building, designed by Erkki Kantonen, Niilo Hartikainen and Jukka Kolehmainen, was built between 1968-1972 and has been listed since 2008. The village also includes subsequent construction from the 1970s, 1990s and most recently 2010-2012.

Originally, the village was infused by the omnipresent spirit of academia created by its community of students and academic staff living in a close-knit neighbourhood, in which Rentukka performed as an important social hub. At present, despite high numbers of students and their activities in the area, the fatigued appearance of the village has been the victim of unstructured and superficial developments.

"Originally, the village was infused by the omnipresent spirit of academia created by its community of students and academic staff living in a close-knit neighbourhood."

Previous page: Kortepohja district pier proposal.
© Aleksandra Zarek

Top: Kortepohja current state
© Aleksandra Zarek

Bottom: Kortepohja promenade proposal.
© Aleksandra Zarek

To revive this dynamic atmosphere, this second scale of rejuvenation aims at consolidating the village through strengthening its circulation and visual perception. The front area, which one is confronted with when arriving from the city centre, lacks strong imagery and a clear sense of orientation. In addition, visual perception of Rentukka as a social hub is currently disturbed by a vast car park, trees and other fragmented additions.

To resolve these issues in this key part of the village, its external spaces have been redefined into new functional zones. This has been achieved by the introduction of a new underground car park, which has freed up space for the insertion of new infrastructure above, including a students' services pavilion, housing blocks and sports areas. Re-establishing the visual presence of Rentukka and its function as a community centre entailed the careful redesign of the approach to the building. It is now served by a prominent landscaped promenade with different surface treatment from the adjacent square.

The previously unused courtyard at the rear is now activated by a new greenhouse pavilion containing a community kitchen, complemented by outdoor growing facilities. These interventions aim at enhancing the existing greenery whilst improving circulation with a new landscaped path, lined with seating arrangements, floor lighting and marking the way to further parts of the village and ultimately to the Rautpohja recreational zone. A new housing cluster has been proposed to replace buildings designated for demolition by the client. The new blocks have their own court and are designed specifically for students with families, being sited in a slightly more removed location with proximity to the recreational Rautpohja zone.

The Rentukka community building, which forms the centrepiece of the historical core of the Kortepohja Student Village, is the subject of the most detailed level of all the interventions undertaken.

Rentukka operated as a vibrant social and cultural centre for the area throughout the decade following its opening in 1972. At the moment its aesthetic appearance, as well as functionality, suffers from its peculiar layout with a rigid grid of columns and numerous partition walls, which has created poorly lit and cramped spaces at all levels. The top floor, which at the peak of the building's former life once served as a chic restaurant, is currently being used only on an extremely occasional basis for social events.

Scale 3:
Rentukka Student
Community Building
retrofit

Rentukka lobby current state.
© Aleksandra Zarek

The fundamental changes proposed to the interior are based on notions of openness, spatial clarity of functions, better light performance and reference to the sculptural appearance of the original building. Due to the heritage status of Rentukka's external envelope, most radical interventions had to be accommodated within the building's shell, which stimulated the creation of tailored design solutions.

Rentukka lobby proposal.
© Aleksandra Zarek

The main concept is based on opening up the ground and top floors to a new atrium, flooded by the light from a generous skylight, which replicates the form of this primary void. A continuous motif in the proposal is the profile of the concrete balustrade, which encircles the volume of the staircase and central void. This proposal, together with the free-form lobby and main skylight, is designed to convey an idea of spatial coherence, undoubtedly lacking in the previous interior layout. The orthogonality of Rentukka's external prisms and it bold columnar grid are now counterbalanced by fluid, curvilinear shapes, which reference Alvar Aalto's architecture across Jyväskylä University and the city.

One side of the atrium is enclosed by a curtain wall to allow light from above to penetrate the volumes of the gym on the top floor and the library on the ground floor. The smooth, white finish of walls and ceilings is designed to maximise reflection of natural light and create a subtle contrast with the warmth of timber elements such as floors, café counter and library shelving.

Student societies, previously scattered throughout the village using temporary arrangements, are now integrated into new functional areas within Rentukka, emphasising its social centrality. Some of them – for example, a new student services desk, cafe, library, gym and open study zone – are placed around the lobby to encapsulate its public atmosphere. The top floor also features a generous group exercise space, art workshops and choir rehearsal space. The separate Lillukka wing now accommodates a cooking club on the ground floor and an auditorium in the basement, which also incorporates a new band rehearsal space.

In order to enhance the clarity of the original volumes, Rentukka's exterior will be cleared of its old superfluous additions. The outdoor area in front of the building is now animated by means of the adjacent new public square and connecting promenade, as shown in the masterplan

Left: Rentukka exterior current state. © Aleksandra Zarek

Right: Rentukka exterior proposal. © Aleksandra Zarek

for the Student Village. This further showcases the consolidated character of the interventions across all scales of development in the Kortepohja district, Student Village and Rentukka.

The three levels of interventions throughout the transformation proposal of Jyväskylä's Kortepohja Student Village formed a comprehensive foundation for its socially-oriented revival. The framework consolidating a development plan for the district, a masterplan for the Student Village and a detailed retrofit of Rentukka acted as a basis for cohesive regeneration, which was built around an integrated and socially sustainable redevelopment strategy.

Recognising the potential of rejuvenation of a single building as a catalyst for integrated regeneration of the area was a key characteristic of the scheme and a crucial driver in conceptualising other development scales to create a multi-dimensional and therefore holistic transformation proposal, which addresses the city's international reputation as a centre for academic excellence and of modernist design by Alvar Aalto. ■

THEIR
TO-
NTIRE
NITY
WHILE
ED.

Houseless
not homeless

By Lavinia Scaletti

"What would an architecture of the houseless be?"

Zip City
Houseless not homeless

By Lavinia Scaletti

London is in the midst of a citywide housing crisis, which, with annual house-building falling short of targets by at least two thirds, shows no signs of ending. For architect Lavinia Scaletti the solution lies not in designing new spaces for living, but in designing new ways of living.

Zip City is an architecture and urban strategy programme exploring a new way of living in cities without a house. Taking London as the site of intervention, it questions whether a possible approach to the city's housing crisis would be to stop building houses and redefine the concepts of ownership, sharing and home.

London is experiencing a housing crisis. With a population of more than 10 million people predicted by 2035 there is an urgent need to provide more homes.[1] As a first response, it seems logical to build more homes to satisfy this growing demand. However, as less than a third of the target number are being built each year, this is a far from viable solution: meaning that more than 300,000 people will be left with no access to housing or experience inadequate living conditions on present estimates.[2] Simultaneously, it could be said that the crisis is caused not by a shortage of built stock but also by the increasing difficulty of accessing this primary resource, usually considered a fundamental right, but which has been compromised by financial speculation and austerity programmes. This is manifested most clearly with new-build apartments and houses that are bought and then lie vacant and unoccupied, removed from their primary and traditional purpose of providing a home.

Speculating upon this near future scenario, Zip City celebrates a new common condition of not having a

Lavinia Scaletti

Lavinia Scaletti is an urban designer and is currently working for Publica, an organisation that specialises in strategies and design for public space, urban design and masterplanning, and is part of a team developing a detailed public realm vision for a key West End street and its surrounding area in London. She trained in architecture at the Royal College of Art and the University of Sheffield. She has previously worked for Koz Architectes in Paris and Elemental in Chile, where she was involved in a variety of public realm and housing projects.

1 This figure is based on numerous newspaper articles and statistics from 2014-2015 estimating that the population in London will be around 10 million people by 2030, taking into account population growth and migration trends.

2 The number is an estimate of the author's for the next 2025 years, based on the relationship between the estimated population number in 2035 and the fact that less than a third of the homes that are needed are built each year. Towards the end of 2014 less than 20,000 new homes were built in London while the building target was between 40,000 – 80,000 new-built homes (numbers depending on who was setting those targets).

dwelling through the implementation of an infrastructure of urban homes. Do we still need houses to live in the city? What would an architecture of the houseless be? And how can we combine the high efficiency that any new urban system requires with our desire for the comforts of a home?

This page (top): Zip Mail: building for mass post boxes. © Lavinia Scaletti

This page (bottom): Zip Eat: multiple microwave structure. © Lavinia Scaletti

To test the viability of such a way of living and to come up with a suitable proposal rather than a predefined theoretical solution, the Zip City programme conducted active research through experiment, focusing on exploring the notion of home and London's evolving living patterns. A ten-day ethnographic experiment of living without a house gave first-hand evidence to better understand the implications arising from a condition of houselessness. The experiment has also helped to define our more "homely" requirements, which are usually taken for granted when living in a fixed location, but which become much more evident when experiencing a nomadic lifestyle. For instance: privacy, technological advancements and the relationship between our bodies and unfamiliar places are some of the issues that have been studied and documented in a research diary. The findings that came out of this initial study have been the prime guide for developing the spatial and programmatic aspects of the proposal.

Section through Zip Storage: multi-functional storage tower for the houseless.
© Lavinia Scaletti

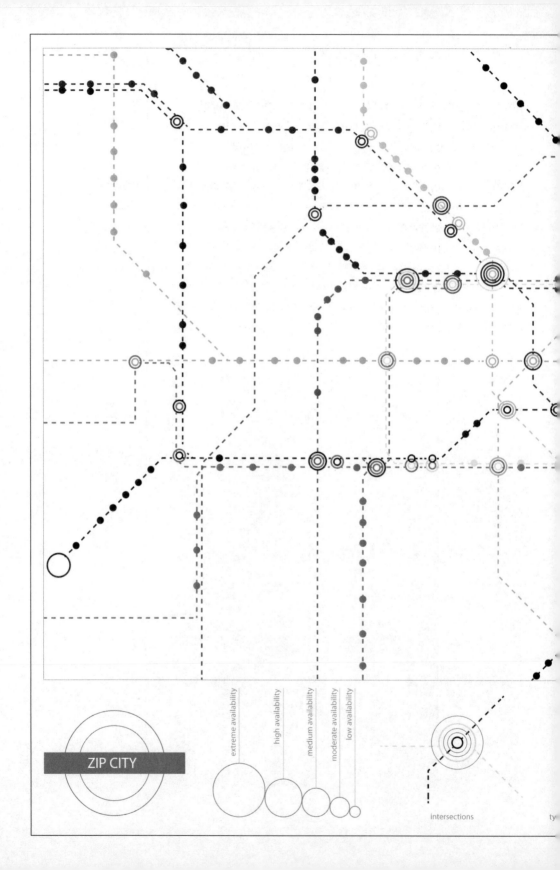

ZIP CITY

extreme availability
high availability
medium availability
moderate availability
low availability

intersections

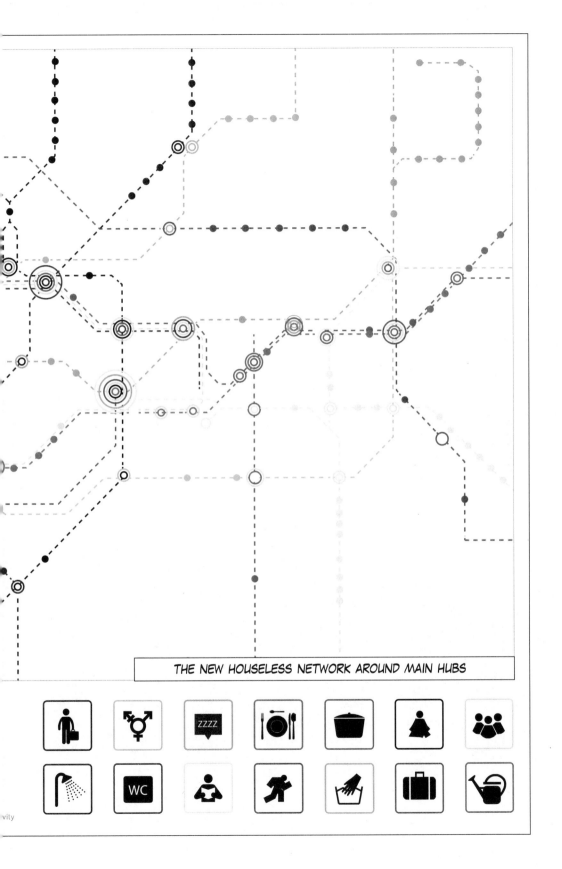

THE NEW HOUSELESS NETWORK AROUND MAIN HUBS

So how is the Zip City proposal grounded in the reality of everyday London and how does this new urban system work, both physically and logistically?

Zip City operates at three scales:

Urban

By moving away from the traditional dwelling, the scheme is first of all conceived at an urban scale, adopting London as the main site for developing the houseless network. Taking advantage of the city's existing and planned infrastructure of transport and services, the new infrastructure of urban homes is located around main transport hubs to allow the new houseless to easily circulate from one Zip place to another and to be fully connected to amenities that are already available in specific areas. In this sense, the project promotes a free lifestyle where one can decide the location for spending time eating, sleeping or doing any other activity.

Architectural

At an architectural level, a system of buildings and spaces designed to fulfill everyday functions are developed around these transport hubs and work within the neighbourhood boundaries. A guide to the architectural typologies for the houseless has been developed using

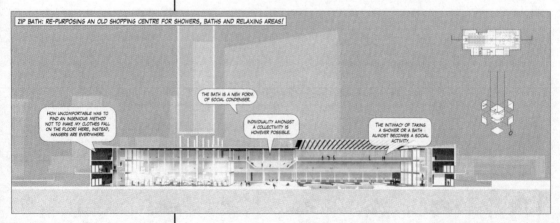

ZIP BATH: RE-PURPOSING AN OLD SHOPPING CENTRE FOR SHOWERS, BATHS AND RELAXING AREAS!

THE BATH IS A NEW FORM OF SOCIAL CONDENSER.

HOW UNCOMFORTABLE WAS TO FIND AN INGENIOUS METHOD NOT TO MAKE MY CLOTHES FALL ON THE FLOOR! HERE, INSTEAD, HANGERS ARE EVERYWHERE.

INDIVIDUALITY AMONGST A COLLECTIVITY IS HOWEVER POSSIBLE.

THE INTIMACY OF TAKING A SHOWER OR A BATH ALMOST BECOMES A SOCIAL ACTIVITY.

the research findings, setting up some general spatial principles that would then be adapted to each specific context. For instance, one of these interventions is a microwave wall, which represents an easy-to-reach food station as well as a new idea of consuming meals better adapted to our current way of eating. Similarly, a new public bath redefines the relationship between private and public for such an intimate activity, and a multifunctional storage tower fulfills its functional purpose, but also creates a space for socialising with other people from the community.

At the furniture scale, a small urban kit provides the basic equipment for the houseless and the possibility of maximum mobility and adaptability. This "piece of home" works in conjunction with the overall system; for example, in the case of the public bath, towels and shampoo are provided, allowing people to carry only the essential everyday items.

Zip City: Houseless not Homeless turns the disadvantaged condition of not having a house into a positive one. It questions the validity of the current ways that home and housing are conceived and proposes an alternative way of inhabiting cities, better suited to our changing patterns of living, to our increasing adaptability to new places and to the development of new technologies.

Zip City promotes a new collective lifestyle where the boundaries between public and private, individual and collective are redefined yet where individual subjectivities can still flourish. ■

Previous page: The new "houseless" network around the main transport hubs of London. © Lavinia Scaletti

Oposite page: Section through Zip Bath: a new communal bathhouse in a converted shopping centre. © Lavinia Scaletti

Furniture

&beyond would like to thank all the *Archifutures Volume 3* contributors, interlocutors and provocateurs, most especially: Aleksandra Zarek; Andrej Strehovec; Felipe de Ferrari, Kim Courreges, Diego Grass, Thomas Batzenschlager of Plan Común; Esen Gökçe Özdamar and Murat Ateş; Guerilla Architects; Ignacio Gias; Jack Self; Jan Glasmeier, a.gor.a architects; Jana Čulek; Lavinia Scaletti; Léopold Lambert; Linnea Våglund and Leo Fidjeland; Manon Mollard; Matias Echanove and Rahul Srivastava of Urbz; Natasha Reid; Nike Kraft; Sara Neves and Filipe Estrela; Ethel Baraona Pohl and César Reyes Nájera; Matevz Čelik and the whole MAO team.

Our thanks also to everyone who has assisted in mapping out the architectural beyond: Annie Åkerman, Brooks Reynolds, Gabriel González, Imgur, Ishan Tankha, Ismini Christakopoulou, Jai Bhadgaonkar, Julien Gregorio, Tang Yuhong and Tiago Ferreirinho.

&beyond
October 2016

Archifutures
Volume 3: The Site
A field guide to making the future of architecture
archifutures.org

A publication series accompanying the Future Architecture platform
futurearchitectureplatform.org

Future Architecture platform is coordinated by
the Museum of Architecture and Design (MAO), Ljubljana
Director Matevž Čelik

Concept, editing and design
&beyond

Editors Rob Wilson, George Kafka, Sophie Lovell, Fiona Shipwright
and Florian Heilmeyer
Design Diana Portela with Janar Siniloo and Lena Giovanazzi

andbeyond.xyz

This book is set in Ergilo, Freight Display and Paul Grotesk
It is printed on Munken Cream 80g paper / Card Graphics 275g
Generated with Print on Demand Technology

First published in 2016
Published by dpr-barcelona in 2016
Viladomat 59 4° 4ª
08015 Barcelona

dpr-barcelona.com

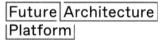

Co-funded by the
Creative Europe Programme
of the European Union

The European Commission support for the production of this publication does not constitute an endorsement of the contents which reflects the views only of the authors, and the Commission cannot be held responsible for any use which may be made of the information contained therein.

Printed in Spain
Legal Deposit: B 26908–2016
ISBN: 978-84-944873-8-5